Christine
Nicholson

EGYPTIAN MAGIC

EGYPTIAN MAGIC

Sir E. A. Wallis Budge

Routledge & Kegan Paul

London and Boston

First published in 1899
by Kegan Paul, Trench, Trübner & Co. Ltd

Reprinted in 1972
by Routledge & Kegan Paul Ltd
Broadway House, 68-74 Carter Lane
London EC4V 5EL and

9 Park Street
Boston, Mass. 02108, U.S.A.

ISBN 0 7100 7200 7

Printed in Great Britain
by Lowe & Brydone (Printers) Ltd, London

PREFACE.

————◆◆————

A STUDY of the remains of the native religious literature of ancient Egypt which have come down to us
has revealed the fact that the belief in magic, that is to
say, in the power of magical names, and spells, and
enchantments, and formulæ, and pictures, and figures,
and amulets, and in the performance of ceremonies
accompanied by the utterance of words of power, to
produce supernatural results, formed a large and
important part of the Egyptian religion. And it is
certain that, notwithstanding the continuous progress
which the Egyptians made in civilization, and the high
intellectual development to which they eventually
attained, this belief influenced their minds and, from
the earliest to the latest period of their history, shaped
their views concerning things temporal as well as
spiritual in a manner which, at this stage in the
history of the world, is very difficult to understand.
The scrupulous care with which they performed their

innumerable religious ceremonies, and carried out the
rules which they had formulated concerning the
worship of the divine Power or powers, and their
devotion to religious magic, gained for them among the
nations with whom they came in contact the reputation
of being at once the most religious and the most
superstitious of men. That this reputation was, on
the whole, well deserved, is the object of this little
book to shew.

Egyptian magic dates from the time when the pre-
dynastic and prehistoric dwellers in Egypt believed
that the earth, and the underworld, and the air, and
the sky were peopled with countless beings, visible and
invisible, which were held to be friendly or unfriendly
to man according as the operations of nature, which
they were supposed to direct, were favourable or
unfavourable to him. In nature and attributes these
beings were thought by primitive man to closely
resemble himself and to possess all human passions,
and emotions, and weaknesses, and defects; and the
chief object of magic was to give man the pre-eminence
over such beings. The favour of the beings who were
placable and friendly to man might be obtained by
means of gifts and offerings, but the cessation of
hostilities on the part of those that were implacable and
unfriendly could only be obtained by wheedling, and

cajolery, and flattery, or by making use of an amulet, or secret name, or magical formula, or figure, or picture which had the effect of bringing to the aid of the mortal who possessed it the power of a being that was mightier than the foe who threatened to do evil to him. The magic of most early nations aimed at causing the transference of power from a supernatural being to man, whereby he was to be enabled to obtain superhuman results and to become for a time as mighty as the original possessor of the power; but the object of Egyptian magic was to endow man with the means of compelling both friendly and hostile powers, nay, at a later time, even God Himself, to do what he wished, whether they were willing or not. The belief in magic, the word being used in its best sense, is older in Egypt than the belief in God, and it is certain that a very large number of the Egyptian religious ceremonies, which were performed in later times as an integral part of a highly spiritual worship, had their origin in superstitious customs which date from a period when God, under any name or in any form, was unconceived in the minds of the Egyptians. Indeed it is probable that even the use of the sign which represents an axe, and which stands as the hieroglyphic character both for God and "god," indicates that this weapon and tool was employed in the

performance of some ceremony connected with religious
magic in prehistoric, or at any rate in predynastic
times, when it in some mysterious way symbolized the
presence of a supreme Power. But be this as it may,
it is quite certain that magic and religion developed
and flourished side by side in Egypt throughout all
periods of her history, and that any investigation which
we may make of the one necessarily includes an
examination of the other.

From the religious books of ancient Egypt we learn
that the power possessed by a priest or man who was
skilled in the knowledge and working of magic was
believed to be almost boundless. By pronouncing
certain words or names of power in the proper manner
and in the proper tone of voice he could heal the sick,
and cast out the evil spirits which caused pain and
suffering in those who were diseased, and restore the
dead to life, and bestow upon the dead man the power
to transform the corruptible into an incorruptible body,
wherein the soul might live to all eternity. His words
enabled human beings to assume divers forms at will,
and to project their souls into animals and other
creatures; and in obedience to his commands, inanimate
figures and pictures became living beings and things
which hastened to perform his behests. The powers of
nature acknowledged his might, and wind and rain,

storm and tempest, river and sea, and disease and
death worked evil and ruin upon his foes, and upon the
enemies of those who were provided with the knowledge of the words which he had wrested from the gods
of heaven, and earth, and the underworld. Inanimate
nature likewise obeyed such words of power, and even
the world itself came into existence through the utterance of a word by Thoth; by their means the earth could
be rent asunder, and the waters forsaking their nature
could be piled up in a heap, and even the sun's course
in the heavens could be stayed by a word. No god,
or spirit, or devil, or fiend, could resist words of power,
and the Egyptians invoked their aid in the smallest as
well as in the greatest events of their lives. To him
that was versed in the lore contained in the books of
the "double house of life" the future was as well
known as the past, and neither time nor distance could
limit the operations of his power; the mysteries of life
and death were laid bare before him, and he could draw
aside the veil which hid the secrets of fate and destiny
from the knowledge of ordinary mortals.

Now if views such as these concerning the magician's
power were held by the educated folk of ancient Egypt
there is little to wonder at when we find that beliefs
and superstitions of the most degraded character
flourished with rank luxuriance among the peasants

and working classes of that country, who failed to understand the symbolism of the elaborate ceremonies which were performed in the temples, and who were too ignorant to distinguish the spiritual conceptions which lay at their root. To meet the religious needs of such people the magician, and in later times the priest, found it necessary to provide pageants and ceremonies which appealed chiefly to the senses, and following their example, unscrupulous but clever men took advantage of the ignorance of the general public and pretended to knowledge of the supernatural, and laid claim to the possession of power over gods, and spirits, and demons. Such false knowledge and power they sold for money, and for purposes of gain the so-called magician was ready to further any sordid transaction or wicked scheme which his dupe wished to carry out. This magic degenerated into sorcery, and demonology, and witchcraft, and those who dealt in it were regarded as associates of the Devil, and servants of the powers of darkness, and workers of the "black art." In the "white" and "black" magic of the Egyptians most of the magic known in the other countries of the world may be found; it is impossible yet to say exactly how much the beliefs and religious systems of other nations were influenced by them, but there is no doubt that certain views and religious ideas of many heathen and

Christian sects may be traced directly to them. Many interesting proofs might be adduced in support of this statement, but the limits of this book will not admit of their being given here.

When we consider the lofty spiritual character of the greater part of the Egyptian religion, and remember its great antiquity, it is hard to understand why the Egyptians carefully preserved in their writings and ceremonies so much which savoured of gross and childish superstition, and which must have been the product of their predynastic or prehistoric ancestors, even during the period of their greatest intellectual enlightenment. But the fact remains that they did believe in One God Who was almighty, and eternal, and invisible, Who created the heavens, and the earth, and all beings and things therein ; and in the resurrection of the body in a changed and glorified form, which would live to all eternity in the company of the spirits and souls of the righteous in a kingdom ruled by a being who was of divine origin, but who had lived upon the earth, and had suffered a cruel death at the hands of his enemies, and had risen from the dead, and had become the God and king of the world which is beyond the grave ; and that, although they believed all these things and proclaimed their belief with almost passionate earnestness, they seem never to have freed themselves from a hankering

after amulets and talismans, and magical names, and
words of power, and seem to have trusted in these to
save their souls and bodies, both living and dead, with
something of the same confidence which they placed in
the death and resurrection of Osiris. A matter for
surprise is that they seem to see nothing incongruous in
such a mixture of magic and religion, and the general
attitude of the mind of the Egyptian, on the point is
well illustrated by the following facts. Attached
to the service of Rā, the Sun-god, at Thebes were
numerous companies of priests whose duties consisted
as much in making copies of religious books and in
keeping alive the " divine traditions," as in ministering
to the god in their appointed seasons. The members of
these companies who wrote the copies of the Book of
the Dead which were buried with kings and queens and
personages of royal or exalted rank declared the power
and omnipotence of Almighty God, Whose visible
emblem to mankind was the Sun, and His sovereignty
over things celestial and things terrestrial with no
uncertain voice, and we should expect them to believe
what they proclaimed, i.e., that God was sufficiently
powerful to protect His emblem in the sky. Yet the
priests of Thebes made copies of works which contained
texts to be recited at specified hours of the day and
night, and gave directions for the performance of

magical ceremonies, the avowed object of such being to prevent the mythical monster Āpep from vanquishing the Sun-god. And it is stated in all seriousness that if a piece of papyrus upon which a figure of the monster has been drawn, and a wax figure of him be burnt in a fire made of a certain kind of grass, and the prescribed words be recited over them as they burn, the Sun-god will be delivered from Āpep, and that neither rain, nor cloud, nor mist shall be able to prevent his light from falling upon the earth. Moreover, the rubric describes the performance of the ceremony as a meritorious act!

E. A. WALLIS BUDGE.

LONDON,
  August 28th, 1899

CONTENTS.

———◆◇◆———

B

LIST OF ILLUSTRATIONS.

———◦✦◦———

EGYPTIAN MAGIC.

CHAPTER I.

ANTIQUITY OF MAGICAL PRACTICES IN EGYPT.

IN the first volume of this series an attempt was made
to set before the reader a statement of the ideas and
beliefs which the ancient Egyptians held in respect of
God, the "gods," the Judgment, the Resurrection, and
Immortality; in short, to sketch in brief outline much
of what was beautiful, and noble, and sublime in their
religion. The facts of this statement were derived wholly
from native religious works, the latest of which is some
thousands of years old, and the earliest of which may
be said to possess an antiquity of between six and seven
thousand years; the extracts quoted in support of the
deductions set forth in it were intended to enable the
reader to judge for himself as to the general accuracy
of the conclusions there given. Many writers on the
Egyptian religion have somewhat blinked the fact that
it had two sides; on the one it closely resembles in

many respects the Christian religion of to-day, and on
the other the religion of many of the sects which
flourished in the first three or four centuries of our era,
and which may be said to have held beliefs which were
part Christian and part non-Christian. In its non-
Christian aspect it represents a collection of ideas and
superstitions which belong to a savage or semi-savage
state of existence, and which maintained their hold in
a degree upon the minds of the Egyptians long after
they had advanced to a high state of civilization. We
may think that such ideas and beliefs are both childish
and foolish, but there is no possible reason for doubting
that they were very real things to those who held them,
and whether they are childish or foolish or both they
certainly passed into the religion of the people of Egypt,
wherein they grew and flourished, and were, at least
many of them, adopted by the Egyptian converts to
Christianity, or Copts. Reference is made to them
in the best classical works of the ancient Egyptians,
and it is more than probable that from them they found
their way into the literatures of the other great nations
of antiquity, and through the Greeks, Romans, Arabs,
and others into the countries of Europe. In the following pages an attempt will be made to place in the
reader's hands the evidence as to the magical side of
the Egyptian religion, which would have been out of
place in the former work, the object of which was
to describe beliefs of a more spiritual nature. But, as

in the book on the Egyptian Ideas of the Future Life, the facts here given are drawn from papyri and other native documents, and the extracts are quoted from compositions which were actually employed by the Egyptians to produce magical effects.

The "magic" of the Egyptians was of two kinds: (1) that which was employed for legitimate purposes and with the idea of benefiting either the living or the dead, and (2) that which was made use of in the furtherance of nefarious plots and schemes and was intended to bring calamities upon those against whom it was directed. In the religious texts and works we see how magic is made to be the handmaiden of religion, and how it appears in certain passages side by side with the most exalted spiritual conceptions; and there can be no doubt that the chief object of magical books and ceremonies was to benefit those who had by some means obtained sufficient knowledge to make use of them. But the Egyptians were unfortunate enough not to be understood by many of the strangers who found their way into their country, and as a result wrong and exaggerated ideas of their religion were circulated among the surrounding nations, and the magical ceremonies which were performed at their funerals were represented by the ignorant either as silly acts of superstition or as tricks of the "black" art. But whereas the magic of every other nation of the ancient East was directed entirely against the powers of darkness, and was

invented in order to frustrate their fell designs by
invoking a class of benevolent beings to their aid, the
Egyptians aimed at being able to command their gods
to work for them, and to compel them to appear at their
desire.   These great results were to be obtained by the
use of certain words which, to be efficacious, must be
uttered in a proper tone of voice by a duly qualified
man; such words might be written upon some substance, papyrus, precious stones, and the like, and worn
on the person, when their effect could be transmitted
to any distance.   As almost every man, woman, and
child in Egypt who could afford it wore some such
charm or talisman, it is not to be wondered at that the
Egyptians were at a very early period regarded as
a nation of magicians and sorcerers.   Hebrew, and
Greek, and Roman writers referred to them as experts
in the occult sciences, and as the possessors of powers
which could, according to circumstances, be employed
to do either good or harm to man.

From the Hebrews we receive, incidentally, it is
true, considerable information about the powers of the
Egyptian magician.   Saint Stephen boasts that the
great legislator Moses "was learned in all the wisdom
"of the Egyptians," and declares that he "was mighty
"in words and in deeds,"[1] and there are numerous
features in the life of this remarkable man which shew
that he was acquainted with many of the practices of

[1] Acts vii. 22.

Egyptian magic. The phrase "mighty in words" probably means that, like the goddess Isis, he was "strong of tongue" and uttered the words of power which he knew with correct pronunciation, and halted not in his speech, and was perfect both in giving the command **and** in saying the word. The turning of a serpent into what is apparently an inanimate, wooden stick,[1] and the turning of the stick back into a writhing snake,[2] are feats which have been performed in the East from the most ancient period; and the power to control and direct the movements of such venomous reptiles was one of the things of which the Egyptian was most proud, and in which he was most skilful, already in the time when the pyramids were being built. But this was by no means the only proof which Moses gives that he was versed in the magic of the Egyptians, for, like the sage Āba-aner and king Necta-nebus, and all the other magicians of Egypt from time immemorial, he and Aaron possessed a wonderful rod[3] by means of which they worked their wonders. At the word of Moses Aaron lifted up his rod and smote the waters and they became blood; he stretched it out

[1] Exodus vii. 10 ff. Two of Moses' opponents were called "Jannes" and "Jambres" (See 2 Timothy iii. 8).

[2] That Moses' rod or serpent should swallow up the rods or serpents of the Egyptians is, of course, to be expected, just as his magical powers are declared to be superior to those of the Egyptians.

[3] An interesting paper on the use of the rod by the Egyptians and Hebrews was published by Chabas in *Annales du Musée Guimet*, tom. i. pp. 35–48, Paris, 1880.

over the waters, and frogs innumerable appeared; when
the dust was smitten by the rod it became lice; and
so on. Moses sprinkled ashes " toward heaven," and
it became boils and blains upon man and beast; he
stretched out his rod, and there was "hail, and fire
"mingled with the hail, very grievous," and the " flax
" and the barley was smitten ; " he stretched out his rod
and the locusts came, and after them the darkness.
Now Moses did all these things, and brought about
the death of the firstborn among the Egyptians by the
command of his God, and by means of the words which
He told him to speak. But although we are told by
the Hebrew writer that the Egyptian magicians could
not imitate all the miracles of Moses, it is quite certain
that every Egyptian magician believed that he could
perform things equally marvellous by merely uttering
the name of one of his gods, or through the words of
power which he had learned to recite; and there are
many instances on record of Egyptian magicians utterly
destroying their enemies by the recital of a few words
possessed of magical power, and by the performance
of some, apparently, simple ceremony.[1] But one great
distinction must be made between the magic of Moses
and that of the Egyptians among whom he lived; the
former was wrought by the command of the God of
the Hebrews, but the latter by the gods of Egypt at
the command of man.

[1] For details, see Chapter III. (Magical Figures).

Later on in the history of Moses' dealings with the Egyptians we find the account of how " he stretched " out his hand over the sea, and the Lord caused the sea " to go *back* by a strong east wind all that night, and " made the sea dry *land*, and the waters were divided. " And the children of Israel went into the midst of the " sea upon the dry *ground*; and the waters *were* a wall " unto them on their right hand, and on their left." When the Egyptians had come between the two walls of water, by God's command Moses stretched forth his hand over the sea, " and the sea returned to his strength," and the " waters returned, and covered the chariots, " and the horsemen, *and* all the host of Pharaoh that " came into the sea after them." [1] But the command of the waters of the sea or river was claimed by the Egyptian magician long before the time of Moses, as we may see from an interesting story preserved in the Westcar Papyrus.[2] This document was written in the early part of the XVIIIth dynasty, about B.C. 1550, but it is clear that the stories in it date from the Early Empire, and are in fact as old as the Great Pyramid. The story is related to king Khufu (Cheops) by Baiu-f-Rā as an event which happened in the time of the king's father, and as a proof of the wonderful powers of magic which were possessed by the priest[3] called

[1] Exodus xiv. 21–28.

[2] See Erman, *Die Märchen des Papyrus Westcar*, Berlin, 1890.

[3] He was the chief *kher heb*, *i.e.*, the head of the priests who officiated in funeral ceremonies, and read the service from a book.

Tchatcha-em-ānkh. It seems that on a certain day king Seneferu was in low spirits, and he applied to the nobles of his royal household expecting that they would find some means whereby his heart might be made glad ; but as they could do nothing to cheer up the king, he gave orders that the priest and writer of books, Tchatcha-em-ānkh, should be brought into his presence immediately, and in accordance with the royal command he was at once brought. When he had arrived, Seneferu said to him, " My brother, I turned " to the nobles of my royal household seeking for some " means whereby I might cheer my heart, but they have " found nothing for me." Then the priest made answer and advised the king to betake himself to the lake near the palace, and to go for a sail on it in a boat which had been comfortably furnished with things from the royal house. " For," said he, " the heart of thy Majesty " will rejoice and be glad when thou sailest about hither " and thither, and dost see the beautiful thickets which " are on the lake, and when thou seest the pretty banks " thereof and the beautiful fields then shall thy heart " feel happiness." He next begged that the king would allow him to organize the journey, and asked his per-mission to let him bring twenty ebony paddles inlaid with gold, and also twenty young virgins having beautiful heads of hair and lovely forms and shapely limbs, and twenty nets wherein these virgins may array themselves instead of in their own ordinary

garments. The virgins were to row and sing to his
Majesty. To these proposals the king assented, and
when all was ready he took his place in the boat;
while the young women were rowing him about hither
and thither the king watched them, and his heart became released from care. Now as one of the young
women was rowing, she entangled herself in some way
in her hair, and one of her ornaments which was made
of "new turquoise" fell into the water and sank; she
ceased to row, and not herself only, but all the other
maidens ceased to row also. When the king saw that
the maidens had ceased from their work, he said to
them, "Will ye not row?" and they replied, "Our
"leader has ceased to row." Then turning to the maiden
who had dropped her ornament overboard, he asked
her why she was not rowing, whereupon she told him
what had happened. On this the king promised that
he would get back the ornament for her.

Then the king commanded that Tchatcha-em-ānkh
should appear before him at once, and as soon as the
sage had been brought into his presence he said to him,
"O Tchatcha-em-ānkh, my brother, I have done
"according to thy words, and the heart of my Majesty
"became glad when I saw how the maidens rowed. But
"now, an ornament which is made of new turquoise and
"belongeth to one of the maidens who row hath fallen
"into the water, and she hath in consequence become
"silent, and hath ceased to row, and hath disturbed the

"rowing of those in her company. I said to her, ' Why
"dost thou not row ?' and she replied, ' An ornament
"[of mine] made of new turquoise hath fallen into the
"water.' Then I said to her, 'I will get it back for
"thee.'" Thereupon the priest and writer of books
Tchatcha-em-ānkh spake certain words of power (*hekau*),
and having thus caused one section of the water of the
lake to go up upon the other, he found the ornament
lying upon a pot-sherd, and he took it and gave it to
the maiden. Now the water was twelve cubits deep,
but when Tchatcha-em-ānkh had lifted up one section
of the water on to the other, that portion became four
and twenty cubits deep. The magician again uttered
certain words of power, and the water of the lake became
as it had been before he had caused one portion of it
to go up on to the other; and the king prepared a feast
for all his royal household, and rewarded Tchatcha-em-
ānkh with gifts of every kind. Such is a story of
the power possessed by a magician in the time of king
Khufu (Cheops), who reigned at the beginning of the
IVth dynasty, about B.C. 3800. The copy of the story
which we possess is older than the period when Moses
lived, and thus there can be no possibility of our seeing
in it a distorted version of the miracle of the waters
of the sea standing like walls, one on the right hand
and one on the left ; on the other hand Moses' miracle
may well have some connexion with that of Tchatcha-
em-ānkh.

Among the Greeks and Romans considerable respect
was entertained, not only for the "wisdom" of the
Egyptians, but also for the powers of working magic
which they were supposed to possess.   The Greek
travellers who visited Egypt brought back to their own
country much information concerning its religion and
civilization, and, though they misunderstood many
things which they saw and heard there, some of the
greatest of thinkers among the Greeks regarded that
country not only as the home of knowledge and the
source of civilization and of the arts, but also as the
fountain head of what has been called " white magic,"
and the "black art."   In some respects they exaggerated
the powers of the Egyptians, but frequently when the
classical writers were well informed they only ascribed
to them the magical knowledge which the Egyptian
magicians themselves claimed to possess.   A striking
instance of this is given in the second book of the
Metamorphoses of Apuleius where, it will be remembered, the following is narrated.   The student Telephron
arrived one day at Larissa, and as he was wandering
about in an almost penniless condition he saw an old
man standing on a large block of stone issuing a
proclamation to the effect that any one who would
undertake to guard a dead body should receive a good
reward.   When Telephron asked if dead men were in
the habit of running away the old man replied testily
to the effect that the witches all over Thessaly used

to tear off pieces of flesh from the faces of the dead
with their teeth, in order to make magical spells by
means of them, and to prevent this dead bodies must
needs be watched at night.   The young man then asked
what his duties would be if he undertook the post, and
he was told that he would have to keep thoroughly
awake all night, to gaze fixedly upon the dead body,
to look neither to the right hand nor to the left, and
not to close the eyes even to wink.   This was absolutely
necessary because the witches were able to get out
of their skins and to take the form of a bird, or dog,
or mouse, and their craftiness was such that they could
take the forms of flies and cast sleep upon the watcher.
If the watcher relaxed his attention and the body
became mutilated by the witches, the pieces of flesh
torn away would have to be made good from the body
of the watcher.   Telephron agreed to undertake the
duty for one thousand nummi, and was led by the old
man to a house, and, having been taken into the room
where the dead body was, found a man making notes
on tablets to the effect that nose, eyes, ears, lips,
chin, etc., were untouched and whole.   Having been
provided with a lamp and some oil that night he began
his watch, and all went well, notwithstanding that he
was greatly afraid, until the dead of night when a
weasel came into the chamber and looked confidingly
at the watcher ; but he drove the animal—which was
no doubt a witch—from the room, and then fell fast

asleep. In the early morning he was suddenly wakened by the trumpets of the soldiers, and almost immediately the widow of the dead man came to him with seven witnesses, and began to examine the body to see if it was intact; finding that no injury had been done to it she ordered her steward to pay Telephron his fee, and was so grateful to him that she promised to make him one of her household. In attempting to express his thanks, however, he made use of some inauspicious words, and immediately the servants of the house fell upon him, and buffeted him, and plucked out his hair by the roots, and tore his clothes, and finally cast him out of the house. Soon afterwards, whilst wandering about, he saw the funeral procession pass through the forum, and at that moment an old man went to the bier, and with sobs and tears accused the widow of poisoning his nephew so that she might inherit his property and marry her lover. Presently the mob which had gathered together wanted to set her house on fire, and some people began to stone her; the small boys also threw stones at her. When she had denied the accusation, and had called upon the gods to be witnesses of her innocence, the old man cried out, "Let, then, Divine Providence decide the truth, in "answer to her denial. Behold, the famous prophet, "Zaclas the Egyptian, dwelleth among us, and he hath "promised me that for much money he will make the "soul of the dead man to return from the place of death

C

"in the underworld, and to make it to dwell in his
"body again for a short time." With these words, he
led forward a man dressed in linen, and wearing palm-
leaf sandals, who, like all the Egyptian priests, had
his head shaved, and having kissed his hands and
embraced his lègs he implored him by the stars, and
by the gods of the underworld, and by the island of
the Nile, and by the Inundation, etc., to restore life
to the dead body, if only for the smallest possible time,
so that the truth of his accusation against the widow
might be proved. Thus adjured Zaclas touched the
mouth and the breast of the dead man three times
with some plant, and having turned his face to the
East and prayed, the lungs of the corpse began to fill
with breath, and his heart to beat, and raising his head
and shoulders he asked why he had been called back
to life, and then he begged to be allowed to rest in
peace. At this moment Zaclas addressed him, and
telling him that he had the power, through his prayers,
to cause the fiends to come and torture him, ordered
him to make known the means by which he had died.
With a groan he replied that the wife whom he had
recently married gave him poison to drink, and that he
died in consequence. The wife at once contradicted the
words of her husband, and of the people who were
standing round some took one side and some another.
At length the husband declared that he would prove
the truth of his own words, and pointing to Telephron,

who had attempted to guard his body, told those
present that the witches after making many attempts
to elude his vigilance had cast deep sleep upon him.
They next called upon himself by his name, which
happened to be Telephron, like that of his watcher,
and whilst he was endeavouring feebly to obey their
spells, his watcher rose up unconsciously and walked
about. Seeing this the witches forced their way into
the room through some unknown place, and having
taken off the nose and ears of the watcher they placed
models of these members in their places. Those who
heard these words looked fixedly at the young man,
who at once put up his hands and touched the members,
whereupon his nose came off in his hand, and his ears
slipped through his fingers on to the ground.

The end of the story does not concern us, and so we
pass on to note that the act of touching the mouth
which Zaclas performed is, of course, a part of the
ceremony of "opening the mouth" which is so often
referred to in religious texts, and was considered of
extreme importance for the welfare of the dead,[1] and
that the power of bringing back the dead to life which
Apuleius ascribes to the priest or magician was actually
claimed some thousands of years before Christ by the
sages of Egypt, as we may see from the following story
in the Westcar Papyrus.

A son of king Khufu (or Cheops, who reigned about

[1] See Chapter VI. (Magical Ceremonies).

B.C. 3800) called Herutātāf, who was famous as a learned
man and whose name is preserved in the " Book of the
Dead" in connection with the "discovery" of certain
Chapters of that wonderful compilation,[1] was one day
talking to his father, presumably on the subject of the
powers of working magic possessed by the ancients.
In answer to some remark by Khufu he replied, " Up
" to the present thou hast only heard reports concerning
" the things which the men of olden time knew, and man
" knoweth not whether they are true or not; but now
" I will cause thy Majesty to see a sage in thine own
" time, and one who knoweth thee not." In reply to
Khufu's question, " Who is this man, O Herutātāf?"
the young man replied, " It is a certain man called
" Teta, who dwelleth in Tet-Seneferu, and is one hundred
" and ten years old, and to this very day he eateth five
" hundred loaves of bread, and the shoulder of an ox, and
" he drinketh one hundred measures of ale. He knoweth
" how to fasten on again to its body a head that hath
" been cut off; he knoweth how to make a lion follow
" him whilst his snare is trailing on the ground; and he
" knoweth the number of the *aptet* of the sanctuary of
" Thoth." Now Khufu had for a long time past sought
out the *aptet* of the sanctuary of Thoth, because he was
anxious to make one similar for his own " horizon."
Though at the present it is impossible to say what the

[1] Chapters **XXX., LXIV., CXXXVII.** See my *Chapters of Coming
Forth by Day* (text), pp. 97, 141, 309.

aptet was, it is quite clear that it was an object or instrument used in. connection with the working of magic of some sort, and it is clear that the king was as much interested in the pursuit as his subjects. In reply to his son's words Khufu told him to go and bring the sage into his presence, and the royal barge or boat having been brought, Herutâtâf set out for the place where the sage dwelt. Having sailed up the river some distance he and his party arrived at Tet-Seneferu, and when the boats had been tied to the quay the prince set out to perform the rest of the journey, which was overland, in a sort of litter made of ebony, which was borne by men by means of poles of *sesnetchem* wood, inlaid with gold. When he had arrived at the abode of Teta, the litter was set down upon the ground, and the prince came out to greet the sage, whom he found lying upon a basket-work bed or mattress, which had been placed for him in the court-yard of his house, whilst one servant shampooed his head, and another rubbed his feet. After a suitable greeting and reference to the sage's honourable condition had been made, Herutâtâf told him that he had come from a great distance in order to bring to him a message from Khufu his father, and the sage bade him "Welcome" heartily, and prophesied that Khufu would greatly exalt his rank. The greetings ended, Herutâtâf assisted Teta to rise, and the old man set out for the quay leaning upon the arm of the king's son, and when he had arrived there he asked that a boat might be provided for the transport of his children and his books. Two boats were at once prepared and filled with their complement of sailors, and Teta sailed down the Nile with Herutātāf, while his family followed.

After a time the party arrived at Khufu's palace, and Herutātāf went into the presence of his father, and reported to him that he had brought Teta the sage for him to see ; Khufu gave orders that he was to be brought before him quickly, and having gone forth into the colonnade of the palace, Teta was led in to him. Khufu said to him, "How is it, Teta, that I have never "seen thee ? " and the sage replied, " O Prince, he who is "called cometh; and since thou hast called me, behold, "here I am." Khufu said to him, "Is it true, according "to what is reported, that thou knowest how to fasten "on again to its body the head which hath been cut "off?" and the sage replied, "Yea, verily, O my lord the "Prince, I do know how to do this thing." And Khufu said, " Let a captive who is shut up in prison be brought "to me so that I may inflict his doom upon him," but Teta made answer, " Nay, my lord the king, let not this "thing be performed upon man, but upon some creature "that belongeth to the sacred animals." Then some one brought to him a goose, and having cut off its head, he laid the body of the goose on the west side of the colonnade, and the head on the east side. Teta then stood up and spake certain words of magical power,

whereupon the body began to move and the head likewise, and each time that they moved the one came
nearer to the other, until at length the head moved to
its right place on the bird, which straightway cackled.
After this Teta had a *khet-āa* bird brought to him, and
upon it he performed the same miracle which he had
wrought upon the goose; and to prove that he had
similar power over the animal creation, an ox was
brought to him, and having cut off its head, which fell
upon the ground, he uttered words of magical power,
and the ox stood up and lived as before.

The two stories from the Westcar Papyrus given
above are sufficient to prove that already in the IVth
dynasty the working of magic was a recognized art
among the Egyptians, and everything we learn from
later texts indicates that it is well-nigh impossible to
imagine a time in Egypt when such was not the case.
But the "wisdom" of the Egyptians was of two kinds,
that is to say, they were possessed of the two kinds
of "wisdom" which enabled them to deal with both
the material world and the spiritual world; the nations
around, however, confused the two kinds, and misunderstood matters in consequence.

One of the oldest names of Egypt is "Kamt" or
"Qemt," a word which means "black" or "dusky,"
and it was applied to the country on account of the
dark colour of the mud which forms the land on each
side of the Nile; the Christian Egyptians or Copts

transmitted the word under the form Khême to the
Greeks, Romans, Syrians, and Arabs. At a very early
period the Egyptians were famous for their skill in
the working of metals and in their attempts to trans-
mute them, and, according to Greek writers, they
employed quicksilver in the processes whereby they
separated the metals gold and silver from the native
ore. From these processes there resulted a " black "
powder or substance which was supposed to possess
the most marvellous powers, and to contain in it the
individualities of the various metals; and in it their
actual substances were incorporated. In a mystical
manner this " black " powder was identified with the
body which the god Osiris was known to possess in
the underworld, and to both were attributed magical
qualities, and both were thought to be sources of
life and power. Thus, side by side with the growth of
skill in performing the ordinary processes of metal-
working in Egypt, there grew up in that country the
belief that magical powers existed in fluxes and alloys;
and the art of manipulating the metals, and the knowledge of the chemistry of the metals and of their
magical powers were described by the name " Khemeia,"
that is to say, " the preparation of the black ore " (or
" powder ") which was regarded as the active principle
in the transmutation of metals. To this name the
Arabs affixed the article *al*, and thus we obtain the
word Al-Khemeia, or Alchemy, which will perpetuate

the reputation of the Egyptians as successful students both of "white magic" and of the "black" art.

But in addition to their skill as handicraftsmen and artisans the Egyptians were skilled in literary composition, and in the production of books, especially of that class which related to the ceremonies which were performed for the benefit of the dead. We have, unfortunately, no means of knowing what early contemporary peoples thought of the Egyptian funeral ceremonies, but it seems to be certain that it was chiefly by means of these that they obtained their reputation as workers of miracles. If by chance any members of a desert tribe had been permitted to behold the ceremonies which were performed when the kings for whom the Pyramids had been built were laid to rest in them, the stories that they took back to their kinsmen would be received as sure proofs that the Egyptians had the power to give life to the dead, to animate statues, and to command the services of their gods by the mere utterance of their names as words of power. The columns of hieroglyphics with which the walls of the tombs were often covered, and the figures of the gods, painted or sculptured upon stelæ or sarcophagi, would still further impress the barbarian folk who always regard the written letter and those who understand it with great awe. The following story from Mas'ûdî [1] will illustrate the views which the Arabs

[1] *Les Prairies d'Or* (ed. by B. de Meynard and P. de Courteille), Paris, 1863, tom. ii. p. 398 f.

held concerning the inscriptions and figures of gods
in the temples of Egypt. It seems that when the
army of Pharaoh had been drowned in the Red Sea,
the women and slaves feared lest they should be
attacked by the kings of Syria and the West; in this
difficulty they elected a woman called Dalūkah as their
queen, because she was wise and prudent and skilled
in magic. Dalūkah's first act was to surround all
Egypt with a wall, which she guarded by men who
were stationed along it at short intervals, her object
being as much to protect her son, who was addicted
to the chase, from the attacks of wild beasts as Egypt
from invasion by nomad tribes; besides this she placed
round the enclosure figures of crocodiles and other
formidable animals. During the course of her reign
of thirty years she filled Egypt with her temples and
with figures of animals; she also made figures of men
in the form of the dwellers in the countries round
about Egypt, and in Syria, and in the West, and of
the beasts which they rode. In the temples she collected all the secrets of nature and all the attracting
or repelling powers which were contained in minerals,
plants, and animals. She performed her sorceries at
the moment in the revolution of the celestial bodies
when they would be amenable to a higher power.
And it came to pass that if an army set out from any
part of Arabia or Syria to attack Egypt, the queen
made the figures of its soldiers and of the animals

which they were riding to disappear beneath the ground,
and the same fate immediately overtook the living
creatures which they represented, wherever they might
be on their journey, and the destruction of the figures
on sculptures entailed the destruction of the hostile
host. In brief, the large figures of the gods which
were sculptured or painted on the walls, and the
hieroglyphic inscriptions which accompanied them,
were considered by those who could neither understand nor read them to be nothing more nor less than
magical figures and formulæ which were intended to
serve as talismans.

The historian Mas'ûdî mentions [1] an instance of the
powers of working magic possessed by a certain Jew,
which proves that the magical practices of the
Egyptians had passed eastwards and had found a
congenial home among the Jews who lived in and
about Babylon. This man was a native of the village
of Zurârah in the district of Kūfa, and he employed
his time in working magic. In the Mosque at Kūfa,
and in the presence of Walīd ibn Ukbah, he raised up
several apparitions, and made a king of huge stature,
who was mounted upon a horsé, gallop about in the
courtyard of the Mosque. He then transformed himself into a camel and walked upon a rope ; and made
the phantom of an ass to pass through his body ; and

[1] *Les Prairies d'Or* (ed. B. de Meynard), Paris, 1865, tom. iv. pp.
266, 267.

finally having slain a man, he cut off the head and removed it from the trunk, and then by passing his sword over the two parts, they united and the man came alive again. This last act recalls the joining of the head of the dead goose to its body and the coming back of the bird to life which has been described above.

We have now to describe briefly the principal means upon which the Egyptians relied for working magic, that is to say, magical stones or amulets, magical figures, magical pictures and formulæ, magical names, magical ceremonies, etc., and such portions of the Book of the Dead as bear upon these subjects generally.

CHAPTER II.

MAGICAL STONES OR AMULETS.

"AMULET" is a name given to a class of objects and ornaments, and articles of dress and wearing apparel, made of various substances which were employed by the Egyptians, and later by other nations, to protect the human body, either living or dead, from baleful influences, and from the attacks of visible and invisible foes. The word "amulet" is derived from an Arabic root meaning "to bear, to carry," hence "amulet" is "something which is carried or worn," and the name is applied broadly to any kind of talisman or ornament to which supernatural powers are ascribed. It is not clear whether the amulet was intended first of all to protect the living or the dead body, but it seems that it was originally worn to guard its owner from savage animals and from serpents. As time went on the development of religious ideas and beliefs progressed, and as a result new amulets representing new views were invented; and the objects which were able to protect the living were made, by an easy transition

in the minds of those who wore them, to protect
the dead.   Moreover, as the preservation of the corruptible body, with the number of its members complete
and intact, was of the most vital importance for the
life of the spiritual and incorruptible body which was
believed to spring therefrom, under the influence of
the new beliefs the dead body became a veritable
storehouse of amulets.   Each member was placed
under the specific protection of some amulet, and a
number of objects which were believed to protect the
body generally from serpents, worms, mildew, decay
and putrefaction were laid·with a lavish hand in, and
upon, and about it, and between the bandages with
which it was swathed.   When men in Egypt began to
lay amulets on their dead cannot be said, and it is
equally impossible to say when the belief in the efficacy
of such and such an amulet sprang into being; it
seems clear, however, that certain amulets represent
beliefs and superstitions so old that even the Egyptians
were, at times, doubtful about their origin and meaning.

Amulets are of two kinds: (1) those which are
inscribed with magical formulæ, and (2) those which
are not.   In the earliest times formulæ or prayers were
recited over the amulets that were worn by the living
or placed on the dead by priests or men set apart to
perform religious services by the community; but it
was not in the power of every man to employ them,
and at a comparatively early date words of magical

power and prayers were cut upon the amulets, which thus became possessed of a twofold power, that is to say, the power which was thought to be inherent in the substance of which the amulet was made, and that which lay in the words inscribed upon it. The earliest name for the formulæ found upon amulets is *hekau*, and it was so necessary for the deceased to be provided with these *hekau*, or " words of power," that in the XVIth century B.C., and probably more than a thousand years earlier, a special section [1] was inserted in the Book of the Dead with the object of causing them to come to him from whatever place they were in, " swifter than greyhounds and quicker than light." The earliest Egyptian amulets known are pieces of green schist, of various shapes, animal and otherwise, which were laid upon the breast of the deceased ; these are found in large numbers in the pre-historic or pre-dynastic graves at several places in Egypt. It is most unlikely that they were made by the aboriginal inhabitants of Egypt, for, notwithstanding the various conjectures which have been made as to their object and use, it is pretty certain that, as M. J. de Morgan said,[2] they "belong to the cult." According to this writer their use was exceedingly widespread until the end of the neolithic period, but with the advent of the

---

[1] *I.e.*, Chapter XXIV., which is entitled, " The Chapter of bringing " words of power unto Osiris in the underworld."

[2] *Ethnographie Préhistorique*, p. 144.

people whom we call Egyptians they become very
rare. In the subsequent period the animal forms disappear, and their place is taken by plaques of schist,
rectangular in shape, upon which are inscribed, in
rough outline, figures of animals, etc. The theory that
these objects were intended as whetstones, or as slabs
upon which to rub down paint, will not hold, for the
reasons which M. J. de Morgan has given. Moreover,
in the green stone scarab which was laid upon the
breast of the deceased in dynastic times, we probably
have a survival of the green schist amulet of pre-
dynastic times in Egypt, both as regards the object
with which it was made and the material. But the
custom of writing *hekau*, or words of power, upon
papyrus is almost as old as that of writing them upon
stone, and we see from the inscription on the walls
of the corridors and chambers of the pyramid of Unas,
king of Egypt about B.C. 3300, that a "book with words
"of magical power" was buried with him.[1] Elsewhere[2] we are told that the book which Teta, king
of Egypt about B.C. 3266, had with him "hath effect
"upon the heart of the gods"; and there is no doubt
that the object of every religious text ever written on
tomb, stele, amulet, coffin, papyrus, etc., was to bring
the gods under the power of the deceased, so that he
might be able to compel them to do his will.

[1] *Unas*, ed. Maspero, line 584.
[2] *Teta*, ed. Maspero, line 351.

1. THE AMULET OF THE HEART, ♡

The heart was not only the seat of the power of life,
but also the source of both good and evil thoughts;
and it sometimes typified the conscience. It was
guarded after death with special care, and was mummified separately, and then, with the lungs, was preserved in a jar which was placed under the protection
of the god Tuamutef. Its preservation was considered
to be of such importance that a text[1] was introduced
into the Book of the Dead at an early period, with
the view of providing the deceased with a heart in the
place of that which had been removed in the process
of mummification. The text reads :—

"May my heart be with me in the House of Hearts!
"May my breast[2] be with me in the House of Hearts!
"May my heart be with me, and may it rest there, or
"I shall not eat of the cakes of Osiris on the eastern
"side of the Lake of Flowers, neither shall I have a
"boat wherein to go down the Nile, nor another wherein
"to go up, nor shall I be able to sail down the Nile
"with thee. May my mouth [be given] to me that
"I may speak therewith, and my two legs to walk
"therewith, and my two hands and arms to overthrow
"my foe. May the doors of heaven be opened unto
"me; may Seb, the prince of the gods, open wide his

[1] Chapter XXVI., entitled, "The Chapter of giving a heart to the
"deceased."

[2] Literally, "pericardium."

D

"two jaws unto me; may he open my two eyes which
"are blindfolded; may he cause me to stretch apart
"my two legs which are bound together; and may
"Anpu (Anubis) make my thighs to be firm so that
"I may stand upon them. May the goddess Sekhet
"make me to rise so that I may ascend into heaven,
"and may that which I command in the House of the
"Ka of Ptah be done. I shall understand with my
"heart, I shall gain the mastery over my heart, I shall
"gain the mastery over my two hands, I shall gain
"the mastery over my legs, I shall have the power to
"do whatsoever my *ka* (*i.e.*, double) pleaseth. My
"soul shall not be fettered to my body at the gates
"of the underworld, but I shall enter in and come
"forth in peace."

When the deceased had uttered these words, it was
believed that he would at once obtain the powers
which he wished to possess in the next world; and
when he had gained the mastery over his heart, the
heart, the double, and the soul had the power to go
where they wished and to do what they pleased. The
mention of the god Ptah and of his consort Sekhet
indicates that the Chapter was the work of the priests
of Memphis, and that the ideas embodied in it are of
great antiquity. According to the Papyrus of Nekhtu-
Amen, the amulet of the heart, which is referred to
in the above Chapter, was to be made of lapis-lazuli,
and there is no doubt that this stone was believed to

possess certain qualities which were beneficial to those
who wore it. It will also be remembered that, according to one tradition,[1] the text of the LXIVth Chapter
of the Book of the Dead was found written in letters
of lapis-lazuli in the reign of Hesep-ti, king of Egypt
about B.C. 4300, and the way in which the fact is
mentioned in the Rubric to the Chapter proves that
special importance was attached to it.

Nefer-uben-f, a priest, guarding his heart against the destroyer of hearts.
(From Naville, *Todtenbuch*, vol. I. plate 39.)

But although a heart might be given to a man by
means of the above Chapter, it was necessary for the
deceased to take the greatest care that it was not
carried off from him by a monster, who was part man
and part beast, and who went about seeking for hearts
to carry away. To prevent such a calamity no less
than seven Chapters of the Book of the Dead (Nos.
XXVII., XXVIII., XXIX., XXIXA, XXX., XXXA,

---

[1] See *Chapters of Coming Forth by Day* (translation, p. 119).

and XXXв) were written. The XXVIIth Chapter
was connected with a heart amulet made of a white,
semi-transparent stone, and reads :—

"Hail, ye who carry away hearts! Hail, ye who
"steal hearts, and who make the heart of a man to go
"through its transformations according to its deeds, let
"not what he hath done harm him before you! Homage
"to you, O ye lords of eternity, ye possessors of ever-
"lastingness, take ye not this heart of Osiris[1] into your
"grasp, and cause ye not words of evil to spring up
"against it; for it is the heart of Osiris, and it belongeth
"unto him of many names,[2] the mighty one whose words
"are his limbs, and who sendeth forth his heart to dwell
"in his body. The heart of Osiris is triumphant, and
"it is made new before the gods: he hath gained power
"over it, and he hath not been judged according to what
"he hath done. He hath gotten power over his own
"members. His heart obeyeth him, he is the lord
"thereof, it is in his body, and it shall never fall away
"therefrom. I, Osiris, victorious in peace, and trium-
"phant in the beautiful Amenta and on the mountain
"of eternity, bid thee [O heart] to be obedient unto
"me in the underworld."

Another Chapter (XXIXв) was connected with a
heart amulet made of carnelian, of which so many
examples may be found in large museums; the text

[1] *I.e.*, the deceased who was identified with Osiris, the god and
judge of the dead.

[2] *I.e.*, Thoth.

reads: "I am the Bennu,[1] the soul of Rā, and the "guide of the gods who are in the underworld. Their "divine souls came forth upon earth to do the will of "their doubles, let therefore the soul of the Osiris come "forth to do the will of his double." The Bennu was also the soul of Osiris, and thus the amulet brought with it the protection of both Osiris and Rā.

But of all the Chapters which related to the heart, the most popular among the Egyptians was that which is commonly known as XXXB, and its importance from a religious point of view cannot be overstated. The antiquity of the Chapter is undoubted, for according to the Papyrus of Nu,[2] a document of the early part of the XVIIIth dynasty, it dates from the time of Hesep-ti, king of Egypt about B.C. 4300, and it seems that it formed a pendant or supplement to the LXIVth Chapter, which professed to give the substance of all the "Chapters of Coming Forth by Day" in a single Chapter. In the rubric to the longer version of the Chapter, given in the same papyrus,[3] Chapter XXXB is connected with Herutātāf, the son of Khufu (Cheops), a man famed for wisdom, and it is there ordered that the words of it be recited over a hard, green stone scarab, which shall be laid in the breast of the deceased where the heart would ordinarily be; this amulet would then perform for him the "opening of the

---

[1] The Bennu bird is usually identified with the phœnix.
[2] Brit. Mus., No. 10,477, sheet 13.   [3] See sheet 21.

"mouth,"[1] for the words of the Chapter would be
indeed "words of power." From reciting the words
of the Chapter over a scarab to engraving them upon
it was but a step, and this step was taken as early
as the IVth dynasty. The text is as follows:—

"My heart, my mother; my heart, my mother! My
"heart whereby I came into being! May naught stand
"up to oppose me at [my] judgment; may there be
"no opposition to me in the presence of the sovereign
"princes; may there be no parting of thee from me
"in the presence of him that keepeth the Balance!
"Thou art my double (ka), the dweller in my body,
"the god Khnemu who knitteth and strengtheneth my
"limbs. Mayest thou come forth into the place of
"happiness whither we go. May the *Shenit*, who form
"the conditions of the lives of men, not make my
"name to stink. Let it be satisfactory unto us, and
"let the listening be satisfactory unto us, and let there
"be joy of heart unto us at the weighing of words.
"Let not that which is false be uttered against me
"before the great god, the lord of Amentet. Verily
"how great shalt thou be when thou risest in triumph."

It was this Chapter which the deceased recited when
he was in the Judgment Hall of Osiris, whilst his
heart was being weighed in the Balance against the
feather symbolic of right and truth. From certain
papyri it seems as if the above words should, properly,

[1] See Chapter VI. (Magical Ceremonies).

be said by the deceased when he is being weighed against his own heart, a conception which is quite different from that of the judgment of the heart before the gods.

The scribe Nebseni being weighed in a balance against his heart in the presence of Osiris. (From the Papyrus of Nebseni, sheet 4.)

2. THE AMULET OF THE SCARAB,

From what has been said above it will be seen that the amulet of the heart, which was connected with the most important and most popular of the Chapters for protecting the heart, was directed to be made in the form of the scarab at a very early date. We can trace the ideas which the Egyptians held about this insect as far back as the time of the building of the Pyramids,[1] and there is no doubt that they represented beliefs which even at that early period were very old. The

[1] King Teta is said to "live like the scarab" (*Teta*, line 89); and again it is said, "Pepi is the son of the Scarab which is born in "Hetepet under the hair of the northern Iusāas" (*Pepi*, line 422).

Egyptian seems to have reasoned thus: since the physical heart is taken from the body before mummification, and the body has need of another to act as the source of life and movement in its new life, another must be put in its place. But a stone heart, whether made of lapis-lazuli or carnelian, is only a stone heart after all, and even though by means of prayers properly recited it prevents the physical heart from being carried off by " those who plunder hearts," it possesses nothing of itself which can be turned to account in giving new life and being to the body on which it lies. But the scarab or beetle itself possesses remarkable powers, and if a figure of the scarab be made, and the proper words of power be written upon it, not only protection of the dead physical heart, but also new life and existence will be given to him to whose body it is attached. Moreover, the scarab was the type and symbol of the god Khepera, the invisible power of creation which propelled the sun across the sky. The particular beetle chosen by the Egyptians to copy for amulets belongs to the family of dung-feeding Lamellicorns which live in tropical countries. The species are generally of a black hue, but amongst them are to be found some adorned with the richest metallic colours. A remarkable peculiarity exists in the structure and situation of the hind legs, which are placed so near the extremity of the body, and so far from each other, as to give the insect a most extraordinary appearance when walking. This peculiar formation is, nevertheless, particularly serviceable to its possessors in rolling the balls of excrementitious matter in which they enclose their eggs. These balls are at first irregular and soft, but, by degrees, and during the process of rolling along, become rounded and harder; they are propelled by means of the hind legs. Sometimes these balls are an inch and a half or two inches in diameter, and in rolling them along the beetles stand almost upon their heads, with the heads turned from the balls. These manœuvres have for their object the burying of the balls in holes, which the insects have previously dug for their reception; and it is upon the dung thus deposited that the larvæ, when hatched, feed. It does not appear that these beetles have the ability to distinguish their own balls, as they will seize upon those belonging to another, in the case of their having lost their own; indeed, it is said that several of them occasionally assist in rolling the same ball. The males as well as the females assist in rolling the pellets. They fly during the hottest part of the day.[1]

Among the ancients several curious views were held about the scarab, whether of the type *scarabæus sacer* or the *ateuchus Ægyptiorum*,[2] and Ælian, Porphyry,

[1] See J. O. Westwood, *Introduction to the Modern Classification of Insects*, London, 1839, vol. i. p. 204 ff.

[2] See my *Mummy*, p. 233.

and Horapollo declared that no female scarab existed.
The last named writer stated that the scarab denoted
"only begotten," because it was a creature self-produced,
being unconceived by a female. He goes on to say
that, having made a ball of dung, the beetle rolls it
from east to west, and having dug a hole, he buries
it in it for eight and twenty days ; on the twenty-ninth
day he opens the ball, and throws it into the water,
and from it the scarabæi come forth. The fact that
the scarab flies during the hottest part of the day
made the insect to be identified with the sun, and the
ball of eggs to be compared to the sun itself. The
unseen power of God, made manifest under the form
of the god Khepera, caused the sun to roll across the
sky, and the act of rolling gave to the scarab its name
kheper, *i.e.*, "he who rolls." The sun contained the
germs of all life, and as the insect's ball contained
the germs of the young scarabs it was identified also
with the sun as a creature which produced life in a
special way. Now, the god Khepera also represented
inert but living matter, which was about to begin a
course of existence, and at a very early period he was
considered to be a god of the resurrection ; and since the
scarab was identified with him that insect became at
once the symbol of the god and the type of the resurrection. But the dead human body, from one aspect,
contained the germ of life, that is to say, the germ
of the spiritual body, which was called into being

by means of the prayers that were recited and the
ceremonies that were performed on the day of the
funeral; from this point of view the insect's egg ball
and the dead body were identical.   Now, as the insect
had given potential life to its eggs in the ball, so, it
was thought, would a model of the scarab, itself the
symbol of the god Khepera, also give potential life to
the dead body upon which it was placed, always provided that the proper "words of power" were first
said over it or written upon it.   The idea of "life"
appears to have attached itself to the scarab from time
immemorial in Egypt and the Eastern Sûdân, for to
this day the insect is dried, pounded, and mixed with
water, and then drunk by women who' believe it to
be an unfailing specific for the production of large
families.   In ancient days when a man wished to drive
away the effects of every kind of sorcery and incantations he might do so by cutting off the head and wings
of a large beetle, which he boiled and laid in oil.
The head and wings were then warmed up and steeped
in the oil of the *āpnent* serpent, and when they had
been once more boiled the man was to drink the
mixture.[1]

The amulet of the scarab has been found in Egypt
in untold thousands, and the varieties are exceedingly
numerous.   They are made of green basalt, green

[1] See Joachim, *Das älteste Buch über Heilkunde*, Berlin, 1890,
p. 160.

granite, limestone, green marble, blue paste, blue glass, purple, blue and green glazed porcelain, etc.; and the words of power are usually cut in outline on the base. In rare instances, the scarab has a human face or head, and sometimes the backs are inscribed with figures of the boat of Rā, of the *Bennu* bird, "the soul of Rā," and of the eye of Horus. The green stone scarabs are often set in gold, and have a band of gold across and

The scribe Ani holding a necklace with pectoral, on which is a figure of the boat of Rā containing a scarab, or beetle, in the presence of Anubis, the god of the dead. (From the *Papyrus of Ani*, plate 15.)

down the back where the wings join; sometimes the whole back is gilded, and sometimes the base is covered with a plate of gold upon which the words of power have been stamped or engraved. Occasionally the base of the scarab is made in the form of a heart, a fact which proves the closeness of the relationship which existed between the amulets of the heart and scarab. In late times, that is to say about B.C. 1200, large funeral scarabs were set in pylon-shaped pectorals, made of porcelain of various colours, upon which the boat of the Sun was either traced in colours or worked in relief, and the scarab is placed so as to appear to be carried in the boat; on the left stands Isis and on the right Nephthys.[1] The oldest green stone funeral scarab known to me is in the British Museum (No. 29,224); it was found at Kûrna near Thebes and belongs to the period of the XIth dynasty, about B.C. 2600. The name of the man for whom it was made (he appears to have been an official of the Temple of Amen) was traced on it in light coloured paint which was afterwards varnished; there are no "words of "power" on this interesting object.

When once the custom of burying scarabs with the bodies of the dead became recognized, the habit of wearing them as ornaments by the living came into fashion, and as a result scarabs of almost every sort and kind may be found by the thousand in many collections, and it is probable that the number of varieties of them was only limited by the ability of those who manufactured them in ancient days to invent new sorts. The use of the scarab amulet passed into Western Asia and into several countries which lay on the Mediterranean, and those who wore it seem to have attached to it much the same idea as its early inventors, the

---

[1] I have given a summary of the chief varieties of the funeral scarab in my *Papyrus of Ani*, London, 1895, p. 262.

Egyptians. From a Greek magical papyrus translated by Goodwin [1] we may see that certain solemn ceremonies were performed over a scarab before it was worn, even in the period of the rule of the Greeks and Romans. Thus about the " ring of Horus " and the " ceremony of the beetle " we are told to take a beetle, sculptured as described below, and to place it on a paper table, and under the table there shall be a pure linen cloth; under it put some olive wood, and set on the middle of the table a small censer wherein myrrh and kyphi shall be offered. And have at hand a small vessel of chrysolite into which ointment of lilies, or myrrh, or cinnamon, shall be put, and take the ring and lay it in the ointment, having first made it pure and clean, and offer it up in the censer with kyphi and myrrh; leave the ring for three days, and take it out and put it in a safe place. At the celebration let there lie near at hand some pure loaves, and such fruits as are in season, and having made another sacrifice upon vine sticks, during the sacrifice take the ring out of the ointment, and anoint thyself with the unction from it. Thou shalt anoint thyself early in the morning, and turning towards the east shalt pronounce the words written below. The beetle shall be carved out of a precious emerald; bore it and pass a gold wire through it, and beneath the beetle carve the

[1] *Fragment of a Græco-Egyptian Work upon Magic* (Publications of the Cambridge Antiquarian Society, 1852).

holy Isis, and having consecrated it as above written, use it. The proper days for the celebration were the 7th, 9th, 10th, 12th, 14th, 16th, 21st, 24th, and 25th, from the beginning of the month; on other days abstain. The spell to be recited began, " I am Thoth, "the inventor and founder of medicines and letters; "come to me, thou that art under the earth, rise up to "me, thou great spirit."

3. THE AMULET OF THE BUCKLE,

This amulet represents the buckle of the girdle of Isis, and is usually made of carnelian, red jasper, red glass, and of other substances of a red colour; it is sometimes made of gold, and of substances covered with gold. It is always associated with the CLVIth Chapter of the Book of the Dead, which is frequently inscribed upon it, and which reads :—

"The blood of Isis, and the strength of Isis, and the "words of power of Isis shall be mighty to act as "powers to protect this great and divine being, and to "guard him from him that would do unto him anything "that he holdeth in abomination."

But before the buckle was attached to the neck of the deceased, where the rubric ordered it to be placed, it had to be dipped in water in which *ānkham* flowers had been steeped; and when the words of the Chapter of the Buckle given above had been recited over it, the amulet brought to the deceased the protection of the blood of Isis, and of her words of power. It will be remembered that she raised the dead body of Osiris by means of her words of power, and there is a legend to the effect that she smote the Sun-god Rā with severe sickness by the magical power which she possessed. Another object of the buckle was to give the deceased access to every place in the underworld, and to enable him to have " one hand towards heaven, and one hand " towards earth."

4. THE AMULET OF THE TET,

This amulet probably represents the tree trunk in which the goddess Isis concealed the dead body of her husband, and the four cross-bars indicate the four cardinal points ; it became a symbol of the highest religious importance to the Egyptians, and the setting up of the Tet at Busiris, which symbolized the re-constituting of the body of Osiris, was one of the most solemn of all the ceremonies performed in connexion with the worship of Osiris. The Tet represents neither the mason's table nor a Nilometer, as some have thought. It is always associated with the CLVth Chapter of the Book of the Dead, which reads :—

" Rise up thou, O Osiris! Thou hast thy backbone, " O Still-Heart ! Thou hast the fastenings of thy neck " and back, O Still-Heart ! Place thou thyself upon

The mummy of Ani the scribe, lying on a bier, attended by Isis, Nephthys, Anubis, the four children of Horus, the *ushabti* figure, his soul, the חَד, etc. (From the *Papyrus of Ani*, plates 33, 34.)

E

"thy base, I put water beneath thee, and I bring unto
"thee a Tet of gold that thou mayest rejoice therein."

Like the buckle, the Tet had to be dipped in the
water in which *ānkham* flowers had been steeped, and
laid upon the neck of the deceased, to whom it gave the
power to reconstitute the body and to become a perfect
KHU (*i.e.*, spirit) in the underworld. On coffins the
right hand of the deceased grasps the buckle, and the
left the Tet; both are made of wood, notwithstanding
the fact that the rubric to the Chapter of the Te
orders the Tet to be made of gold.

5. THE AMULET OF THE PILLOW, ⏾

This amulet is a model of the pillow which is found
placed under the neck of the mummy in the coffin, and
its object is to "lift up" and to protect the head of the
deceased; it is usually made of hæmatite, and is
inscribed with the text of the CLXVIth Chapter of the
Book of the Dead, which reads :—

"Thou art lifted up, O sick one that liest prostrate.
"They lift up thy head to the horizon, thou art raised
"up, and dost triumph by reason of what hath been
"done for thee. Ptah hath overthrown thine enemies,
"which was ordered to be done for thee. Thou art
"Horus, the son of Hathor, . . . who givest back the
"head after the slaughter. Thy head shall not be
"carried away from thee after [the slaughter], thy head
"shall never, never be carried away from thee."

6. The Amulet of the Vulture,

This amulet was intended to cause the power of Isis as the " divine mother " to be a protection for the deceased, and was made of gold in the form of a vulture hovering in the air with outstretched wings and holding in each talon the symbol of " life " ♀, and was placed on the neck on the day of the funeral. With this amulet the CLVIIth Chapter of the Book of the Dead was associated, and it was ordered by the rubric to it to be recited over it; this text reads :—

" Isis cometh and hovereth over the city, and she " goeth about seeking the secret habitations of Horus " as he emergeth from his papyrus swamps, and she " raiseth up his shoulder which is in evil case. He is " made one of the company in the divine boat, and the " sovereignty of the whole world is decreed for him. " He hath warred mightily, and he maketh his deeds to " be remembered; he hath made the fear of him to " exist and awe of him to have its being. His mother " the mighty lady, protecteth him, and she hath " transferred her power unto him." The first allusion is to the care which Isis shewed for Horus when she was bringing him up in the papyrus swamps, and the second to his combat with Set, whom he vanquished through the might of Isis.

7. THE AMULET OF THE COLLAR OF GOLD, 〜

This amulet was intended to give the deceased power to free himself from his swathings ; it is ordered by the rubric to the CLVIIIth Chapter of the Book of the Dead to be placed on his neck on the day of the funeral, and to be made of gold. The text of the Chapter reads:—"O my father, my brother, my mother Isis, "I am unswathed, and I see. I am one of those who "are unswathed and who see the god Seb." This amulet is very rare, and appears to have been the expression of beliefs which grew up in the period of the XXVIth dynasty, about B.C. 550.

8. THE AMULET OF THE PAPYRUS SCEPTRE, ⎰

This amulet was intended to give the deceased vigour and renewal of youth; it was made of mother-of-emerald, or of light green or blue porcelain, and, when the words of the CLIXth Chapter of the Book of the Dead had been recited over it, it was placed on his neck on the day of the funeral. In the XXVIth dynasty and later it seems as if the amulet represented the power of Isis, who derived it from her father, the husband of Renenet, the goddess of abundant harvests and food. At an earlier period, judging from the text of the CLXth Chapter, the amulet is put by the god

Thoth into the hands of the deceased, who says, " It is
"in sound state, and I am in sound state; it is not
"injured, and I am not injured; it is not worn away,
"and I am not worn away."

9. THE AMULET OF THE SOUL,

This amulet was made of gold inlaid with precious
stones in the form of a human-headed hawk, and,
when the words of the LXXXIXth Chapter of the
Book of the Dead had been recited over it, it was
directed by the rubric to the Chapter to be placed
upon the breast of the deceased. The object of the
amulet is apparent from the text in which the deceased
is made to say, " Hail, thou god Anniu ! Hail, thou
"god Pehrer, who dwellest in thy hall ! Grant thou
"that my soul may come unto me from wheresoever
"it may be. If it would tarry, then let my soul
"be brought unto me from wheresoever it may be. ...
"Let me have possession of my soul and of my
"spirit, and let me be true of voice with them
"wheresoever they may be. . . . Hail, ye gods, who
"tow along the boat of the lord of millions of years,
"who bring it above the underworld, and who make it
"to travel over Nut, who make souls to enter into their
"spiritual bodies, ... grant that the soul of the Osiris[1]

---

[1] *I.e.*, the deceased, who is identified with the god Osiris.

"may come forth before the gods, and that it may be
"true of voice with you in the east of the sky, and
"follow unto the place where it was yesterday, and
"enjoy twofold peace in Amentet. May it look upon
"its natural body, may it rest upon its spiritual body,
"and may its body neither perish nor suffer corruption
"for ever!" Thus the amulet of the soul was intended
to enable the soul both to unite with the mummified
body, and to be with its spirit (*khu*) and spiritual body
at will.

10. THE AMULET OF THE LADDER,

In tombs of the Ancient and Middle Empires small
objects of wood and other substances in the form of
ladders have often been found, but the signification of
them is not always apparent. From the texts inscribed upon the walls of the corridors and chambers
of the pyramids of Unas, Teta, Pepi, and other early
kings, it is clear that the primitive Egyptians believed
that the floor of heaven, which also formed the sky of
this world, was made of an immense plate of iron, rectangular in shape, the four corners of which rested upon
four pillars which served to mark the cardinal points.
On this plate of iron lived the gods and the blessed
dead, and it was the aim of every good Egyptian to go
there after death. At certain sacred spots the edge of

the plate was so near the tops of the mountains that
the deceased might easily clamber on to it and so
obtain admission into heaven, but at others the distance
between it and the earth was so great that he needed
help to reach it.   There existed a belief that Osiris
himself experienced some difficulty of getting up to
the iron plate, and that it was only by means of the
ladder which his father Rā provided that he at length
ascended into heaven.   On one side of the ladder stood
Rā, and on the other stood Horus,[1] the son of Isis, and
each god assisted Osiris to mount it.   Originally the
two guardians of the ladder were Horus the Elder and
Set, and there are several references in the early texts
to the help which they rendered to the deceased, who
was, of course, identified with the god Osiris.   But,
with a view either of reminding these gods of their
supposed duty, or of compelling them to do it, the
model of a ladder was often placed on or near the dead
body in the tomb, and a special composition was
prepared which had the effect of making the ladder
become the means of the ascent of the deceased into
heaven.   Thus in the text written for Pepi [2] the
deceased is made to address the ladder in these words :
" Homage to thee, O divine Ladder !   Homage to
" thee, O Ladder of Set !   Stand thou upright, O divine
" Ladder !   Stand thou upright, O Ladder of Set !   Stand
" thou upright, O Ladder of Horus, whereby Osiris

---

[1] *Unas*, line 579.   [2] Line 192 f.

" came forth into heaven when he made use of his
" magical power upon Rā. . . . For Pepi is thy son,
" and Pepi is Horus, and thou hast given birth unto
" Pepi even as thou hast given birth unto the god who
" is the lord of the Ladder (*i.e.*, Horus) ; and thou shalt
" give unto Pepi the Ladder of the god (*i.e.*, Horus), thou
" shalt give unto him the Ladder of the god Set whereby
" this Pepi shall come forth into heaven when he shall
" have made use of his magical power upon Rā.   O
" thou god of those whose doubles (*kau*) pass onwards,
" when the Eye of Horus soareth upon the wing of
" Thoth on the east side of the divine Ladder (*or*
" Ladder of God), O men whose bodies [would go]
" into heaven, Pepi is the Eye of Horus, and when the
" Eye turneth itself to any place where he is, Pepi
" goeth side by side with the Eye of Horus, and O
" ye who are the brethren of the gods, rejoice ye that
" Pepi journeyeth among you.   And the brethren of
" Pepi who are the gods shall be glad when they meet
" Pepi, even as Horus is glad when he meeteth his
" Eye.   He hath placed his Eye before his father Seb,
" and every god and every spirit stretcheth out his
" hand towards Pepi when he cometh forth into heaven
" from the Ladder.   Pepi hath need neither to ' plough
" the earth,' nor to ' collect the offering ' ; and he hath
" need neither to go to the Hall which is in Annu
" (Heliopolis), nor to the Hall of the Morning which is
" in Annu ; for that which he seeth and that which he

" heareth shall feed him and nourish him when he
" appeareth in heaven from the Ladder. Pepi riseth
" like the uraeus on the forehead of Set, and every
" god and every spirit stretcheth out his hand to Pepi
" on the Ladder. Pepi hath gathered together his
" bones, he hath collected his flesh, and he hath gone
" quickly into heaven by means of the two fingers [1]
" of the god of the Ladder (*i.e.*, Horus)." Elsewhere [2]
the gods Khonsu, Sept, etc., are invoked to bring the
ladder to Pepi, and the ladder itself is adjured to
come with its name, and in another place [3] we read,
" Homage to thee, O thou Ladder that supportest the
" golden vase of the Spirits of Pe and the Spirits of
" Nekhen, stretch out thy hand to this Pepi, and let
" him take his seat between the two great gods who
" are in the place of this Pepi ; take him by the hand
" and lead him towards Sekhet-Hetep (*i.e.*, the Elysian
" Fields), and let him take his seat among the stars
" which are in the sky."

In the Theban Recension of the Book of the Dead
the importance of the ladder is also seen, for in
Chapter CXLIX. [4] the deceased says, " I set up a
" Ladder among the gods, and I am a divine being
" among them " ; and in Chapter CLIII. he says, " The

[1] Compare, " Give thou to Pepi these two fingers which thou hast
"given to Nefert, the daughter of the great god, as messengers from
"heaven to earth " (*Pepi*, line 422).

[2] *Pepi*, line 200.   [3] *Pepi*, line 471.

[4] See my *Chapters of Coming Forth by Day*, translation, p. 270.

" Osiris Nu shall come forth upon your Ladder which
" Rā hath made for him, and Horus and Set shall grasp
" him firmly by the hand." Finally, when the custom
of placing a model of the ladder in the tomb fell into
disuse, the priests provided for the necessity of the
dead by painting a ladder on the papyri that were
inscribed with the texts from the Book of the Dead
and were buried with them.[1]

11. THE AMULET OF THE TWO FINGERS,

This amulet is intended to represent the two fingers,
index and medius, which the god Horus employed in
helping his father Osiris up the ladder[2] into heaven,
as has been described above ; it is found in the interior
of mummies and is usually made of obsidian or
hæmatite.

12. THE AMULET OF THE EYE OF HORUS,

The Eye of Horus amulet, or Utchat, is one of the
commonest of all, and its use seems to have been
universal at all periods. It was made of gold, silver,
granite, hæmatite, carnelian, lapis-lazuli, porcelain,
wood, etc., although the rubric of a late Chapter
of the Book of the Dead[3] directs that the amulet

---

[1] See the *Papyrus of Ani*, 2nd edition, pl. 22.
[2] See *Pepi*, line 196.   [3] *I.e.*, CXL.

should be made either of lapis-lazuli or of *mak* stone. The Utchat is of two kinds, one facing to the left and the other to the right, and together they represent the two eyes of Horus, one of which, according to an ancient text, was white and the other black; from another point of view one Utchat represents the Sun and the other the Moon, or Rā and Osiris respectively. But speaking generally, when the Egyptians wore the Utchat as an amulet they intended it to bring to them the blessings of strength, vigour, protection, safety, good health, and the like, and they had in their minds the Eye of Horus, probably the white one, or the Sun. In religious texts the expression *meh Utchat, i.e.*, the "filling of the Utchat," is often used, and from many considerations it is clear that we must understand it to refer to the Sun at the summer solstice; thus the amulet seems to have been intended to bring to its wearer strength and health similar to that of the Sun at the season of the year when it is most powerful. In the CLXVIIth Chapter of the Book of the Dead the deceased is made to say, " The god Thoth hath brought "the Utchat, and he hath made it to rest after it "departed, O Rā. It was grievously afflicted by the "storm, but Thoth made it to rest after it departed "out of the storm. I am sound, and it is sound; I "am sound, and it is sound; and Nebseni, the lord of "piety, is sound." To obtain the full benefit of the Utchat amulet for the deceased it was obligatory to

make one in lapis-lazuli and to plate it with gold,
and then to offer to it offerings at the summer solstice;
another had then to be made of jasper and, if after
the specified Chapter (CXL.) had been recited over it,
it was laid on any part of the body of the deceased,
he would become a god and take his place in the boat
of Rā. At this solstice twelve altars[1] had to be
lighted, four for Rā-Temu, four for the Utchat, and
four for the other gods who had been mentioned in
the Chapter. An interesting example of the use of the
utchat occurs in a Greek spell for the discovery of a
thief written as late as the IVth century of our era.[2]
In it we are told to "take the herb *khelkbei* and *bugloss*,
"press out the juice and burn the crushed leaves and
"mix the ashes with the juice. Anoint and write
"upon a wall Khoō with these materials. And take
"a common piece of wood, and cut a hammer out of
"it, and strike with it upon the ear, pronouncing this
"spell:—'I adjure thee by the holy names, render up
"the thief, who has carried away such [and such] a
"thing Khalkhak, Khalkoum, Khiam, Khar, Khroum,
"Zbar, Bēri, Zbarkom, Khrē, Kariōb, Pharibou, and by
"the terrible names αεεηηηιιιοοοοουυυυυνωωωωωωω.'"[3]
Following these words we have a picture of the *utchat*

---

[1] One for each month of the year.

[2] Kenyon, *Catalogue of Greek Papyri*, p. 64.

[3] The seven vowels were supposed in the Gnostic system to contain
all the names of God, and were, therefore, most powerful when used
as a spell.

with an arrangement of certain vowels on each side of
it thus :—

ω	a
υυ	εε
ιιι	ηηη
ηηηηη	ιιι
εεεεεε	ηηηηη
aaaaaaa	εεεεεε
	aaaaaaa

The spell continues, "'Render up the thief who has
"stolen such [and such] a thing : as long as I strike
"the ear with this hammer, let the eye of the thief
"be smitten and inflamed until it betrays him.' Saying
"these words strike with the hammer." [1]

13. THE AMULET OF "LIFE," ☥ (ĀNKH).

The object which is represented by this amulet is
unknown, and of all the suggestions which have been
made concerning it none is more unlikely than that
which would give it a phallic origin. Whatever it
may represent, it certainly symbolizes "life"; every
god carries it, and it seems, even in the earliest times,
to be a conventional representation of some object
which in the remotest period had been used as an
amulet. In the Papyrus of Ani (2nd edit.,
plate 2) the Ānkh rises from the Tet, and the
arms which project from it support the disk of
the sun as here seen. This amulet is made of

[1] See Goodwin, *Fragment of a Græco-Egyptian work upon Magic*, p. 7.

various substances, and was chiefly employed as a
pendant of a necklace.

14. THE AMULET NEFER,

This amulet signifies "happiness, good luck," etc.,
and represents a musical instrument; it was made
of carnelian, red stone, red porcelain, and the like,
and was a very favourite form for the pendants of
necklaces and strings of beads.

15. THE AMULET OF THE SERPENT'S HEAD,

This amulet was placed on the dead body to keep
it from being bitten by snakes in the underworld or
tomb. It is made of red stone, red jasper, red paste,
and carnelian. As the goddess Isis is often typified
by a serpent, and red is a colour peculiar to her, it
seems as if the idea underlying the use of this amulet
was to vanquish the snakes in the tomb by means of
the power of the great snake-goddess Isis. This power
had been transferred to it by means of the words of
the XXXIVth Chapter of the Book of the Dead,
which are often inscribed upon it. The text reads:—
"O Serpent! I am the flame which shineth upon the
"Opener of hundreds of thousands of years, and the
"standard of the god Tenpu," or as others say,
"the standard of young plants and flowers. Depart
"ye from me, for I am the divine Lynx." Some

have thought that the snake's head represents the serpent which surmounts the ram's head on the *urhekau* instrument used in performing the ceremony of " Opening the mouth." [1]

The Kher-heb priest touching the statue of the deceased with the *urhekau* instrument to effect the " opening of the mouth." (From the *Papyrus of Ani*, plate 15.)

16. THE AMULET OF THE MENAT,

This amulet was in use in Egypt as early as the VIth dynasty, and it was worn or held or carried with the sistrum by gods, kings, priests, priestesses, etc.; usually it is held in the hand, but it is often worn on the neck. Its object was to bring joy and health to the wearer, and it was believed to possess magical properties; it represented nutrition [2] and

---

[1] See the description of this ceremony in Chapter VI.

[2] *Menat* is connected with the root from which the word for " nurse " (*menāt*) is derived ; see the article by Lefébure, " Le Menat et le Nom " de l'Eunuque" in *Proc. Soc. Bibl. Arch.*, 1891, p. 333 f.

strength, and the might of the male and female organs of generation, mystically considered, was supposed to be united therein. The amulet is made in bronze, stone, porcelain, and other substances, and when laid upon the body of the dead brought to it the power of life and reproduction.

17. THE AMULET OF THE SAM,

This amulet is probably intended to represent an organ of the human body, and its use is very ancient; it is made of lapis-lazuli and other hard stone substances, and in the late period is often found in the swathings of mummies. Its primary meaning is "union," and refers to animal pleasure.

18. THE AMULET OF THE SHEN, Ω

This amulet is intended to represent the sun's orbit, and it became the symbol of an undefined period of time, i.e., eternity; it was laid upon the body of the dead with the view of giving to it life which should endure as long as the sun revolved in its orbit in the heavens. In the picture of the mummy chamber[1] the goddesses Isis and Nephthys are seen kneeling and resting their hands on *shen*. Figures of the *shen* were

[1] See *Papyrus of Ani*, 2nd edit., plates 33, 34.

F

painted upon stelæ, coffins, etc.; as an amulet it is commonly made of lapis-lazuli or carnelian. The amulet of the cartouche ⬭ has been supposed to be nothing more than *shen* elongated, but it probably refers to the ordinary meaning of ⬭ *i.e.*, "name."

19. The Amulet of the Steps, ⌐⌐

This amulet seems to have two meanings: to lift up to heaven, and the throne of Osiris. According to one legend, when the god Shu wished to lift up the goddess Nut from the embrace of the god Seb, so that her body, supported by her stretched-out arms and legs, might form the sky, he found that he was not tall enough to do so; in this difficulty he made use of a flight of steps, and having mounted to the top of these he found himself able to perform his work. In the fourth section of the Elysian Fields [1] three such flights of steps are depicted. In the XXIInd Chapter of the Book of the Dead the deceased prays that he "may "have a portion with him who is on the top of the "steps," *i.e.*, Osiris, and in funeral vignettes this god is seen seated upon the top of a flight of steps and holding his usual symbols of sovereignty and dominion. The amulet of the Steps is usually made of green or blue glazed porcelain.

[1] See *Papyrus of Ani*, 2nd edit., plate 35.

20. The Amulet of the Frog,

This amulet is typical of teeming life and of the resurrection. The frog-headed goddess Heqt, the wife of Khnemu, was associated with the resurrection, and this amulet, when laid upon the body of the dead, was intended to transfer to it her power. The frog is often represented on the upper part of the Greek and Roman terra-cotta lamps which are found in Egypt, and on one of them written in Greek is the legend, " I am the " resurrection." [1]

The amulets described above are those which are most commonly found in the tombs and on mummies, but a few others are also known, e.g., the White crown of the South, the Red crown of the North, the horizon, or place where the sun rises, an angle, typifying protection, the horns, disk, and plumes, or the plummet, etc. Besides these, any ring, or pendant, or ornament, or any object whatsoever, upon which was inscribed the name of a god or his emblem, or picture, became an amulet with protective powers; and it seems that these powers remained active as long as the substance lasted and as long as the name, or emblem, or picture, was not

[1] See Lanzone, *Dizionario*, p. 853.

erased from it. The use of amulets was common in Egypt from the earliest times to the Roman Period, and when the Egyptians embraced Christianity, they, in common with the Gnostics and semi-Christian sects, imported into their new faith many of the views and beliefs which their so-called heathen ancestors had held, and with them the use of the names of ancient Egyptian gods, and goddesses, and demons, and formulæ, which they employed in much the same way as they were employed in the days of old.

CHAPTER III.

MAGICAL FIGURES.

IT has been said above that the name or the emblem
or the picture of a god or demon could become an
amulet with power to protect him that wore it, and
that such power lasted as long as the substance of
which it was made lasted, if the name, or emblem, or
picture was not erased from it.   But the Egyptians
went a step further than this, and they believed that
it was possible to transmit to the *figure* of any man,
or woman, or animal, or living creature, the soul of
the being which it represented, and its qualities and
attributes.   The statue of a god in a temple contained
the spirit of the god which it represented, and from
time immemorial the people of Egypt believed that
every statue and every figure possessed an indwelling
spirit.   When the Christianized Egyptians made their
attacks on the "idols of the heathen" they proved
that they possessed this belief, for they always endeavoured to throw down the statues of the gods of

the Greeks and Romans, knowing that if they were
once shattered the spirits which dwelt in them would
have no place wherein to dwell, and would thereby
be rendered homeless and powerless. It will be remembered that it is stated in the Apocryphal Gospels
that when the Virgin Mary and her Son arrived in
Egypt there " was a movement and quaking throughout
" all the land, and all the idols fell down from their
" pedestals and were broken in pieces." Then all the
priests and nobles went to a certain priest with whom
" a devil used to speak from out of the idol," and they
asked him the meaning of these things; and when he
had explained to them that the footstep of the son
of the "secret and hidden god" had fallen upon the
land of Egypt, they accepted his counsel and made a
figure of this god. The Egyptians acknowledged that
the new god was greater than all their gods together,
and they were quite prepared to set up a statue of him
because they believed that in so doing they would
compel at least a portion of the spirit of the "secret
and hidden god" to come and dwell in it. In the
following pages we shall endeavour to describe the
principal uses which the Egyptians made of the figures
of gods, and men, and beasts, to which magical powers
had been imparted by means of the performance of
certain symbolic ceremonies and the recital of certain
words of power; and how they could be employed to
do both good and evil.

One of the earliest instances of the use of a magical figure is related in the Westcar Papyrus,[1] where we read that Prince Khāf-Rā told Khufu (Cheops) a story of an event which had happened in the time of Neb-ka or Neb-kau-Rā, a king of the IIIrd dynasty, who reigned about B.C. 3830. It seems that this king once paid a visit to one of his high officials called Āba-aner, whose wife fell violently in love with one of the soldiers in the royal train. This lady sent her tire-woman to him with the gift of a chest of clothes, and apparently she made known to him her mistress's desire, for he returned with her to Āba-aner's house. There he saw the wife and made an appointment to meet her in a little house which was situated on her husband's estate, and she gave instructions to one of the stewards of Āba-aner to prepare it for the arrival of herself and her lover. When all had been made ready she went to the house and stayed there the whole day drinking and making love with the man until sunset; and when the evening had come he rose up and went down to the river and the tirewoman bathed him in the water thereof. But the steward, who had made ready the house, declared that he must make the matter known unto his master, and on the following morning as soon as it was light, he went to Āba-aner and related to him everything which had happened. The official made no answer to his

[1] Ed. Erman, pp. 7 and 8.

servant's report, but ordered him to bring him certain
materials and his box made of ebony and precious
metal. Out of the box he took a quantity of wax,
which was, no doubt, kept there for purposes similar
to that to which a portion of it was now to be put,
and made a model of a crocodile seven spans long,
and then reciting certain magical words over it, he
said, "When the man cometh down to bathe in
"my waters seize thou him." Then, turning to the
steward, he gave the wax crocodile to him and said,
"When the man, according to his daily wont,
"cometh down to wash in the water thou shalt cast
"the crocodile in after him"; and the steward
having taken the wax crocodile from his master went
his way.

And again the wife of Āba-aner ordered the steward
who had charge of the estate to make ready the house
which was in the garden, "for," she said, "behold, I
"am coming to pass some time therein." So the house
was made ready and provided with all good things,
and she came with the man and passed some time
with him there. Now when the evening was come
the man went down to the water to wash according to
his daily wont, and the steward went down after him
and threw into the water the wax crocodile, which
straightway turned into a living crocodile seven cubits
(*i.e.*, about twelve feet) in length, and seized upon the
man and dragged him down in the water.

Meanwhile Āba-aner tarried with his king Neb-kau-Rā for seven days, and the man remained in the depths of the water and had no air to breathe. And on the seventh day Āba-aner the *kher heb*[1] went out with the king for a walk, and invited His Majesty to come and see for himself a wonderful thing which had happened to a man in his own days; so the king went with him. When they had come to the water Āba-aner adjured the crocodile, saying, " Bring hither the man," and the crocodile came out of the water bringing the man with him. And when the king remarked that the crocodile was a horrid looking monster, Āba-aner stooped down and took it up into his hand, when it straightway became a waxen crocodile as it was before. After these things Āba-aner related to the king what had happened between his wife and the man whom the crocodile had brought up out of the water, where-upon the king said to the crocodile, " Take that which "is thine and begone"; and immediately the crocodile seized the man and sprang into the water with him, and disappeared in its depths. And by the royal command Āba-aner's wife was seized, and having been led to the north side of the palace was burnt, and her ashes were cast into the stream. Here then we have already in the IIIrd dynasty the existence of a belief that a wax crocodile, over which certain words

---

[1] *I.e.*, the priestly official who performed the most important of the funeral ceremonies; he was always a man of great learning, and generally of high rank.

had been said, could change itself into a living reptile at pleasure, and that a man could be made by the same means to live at the bottom of a stream for seven days without air. We may also notice that the great priestly official, the *kher heb*, was so much in the habit of performing such acts of magic that he kept in a room a box of materials and instruments always ready for the purpose; and, apparently, neither himself, nor his king, nor his servant, thought the working of magic inconsistent with his high religious office.

But at the time when Āba-aner was working magic by means of wax figures, probably to the harm and injury of his enemies, the priests were making provision for the happiness and well-being of the dead also by means of figures made of various substances. According to one very early belief the dead made their way to a region called Sekhet-Aaru, where they led a life which was not very different from that which they had led upon earth. From the pictures of this place which are painted on coffins of the XIth dynasty, we see that it was surrounded by streams of water, and that it was intersected by canals, and that, in fact, it was very much like an ordinary well-kept estate in the Delta. The beings who lived in this place, however, had the same wants as human beings, that is to say, they needed both food and drink, or bread-cakes and ale. The existence of bread and ale presupposed the existence of wheat and barley, and

the production of these presupposed the tilling of the
ground and the work of agricultural labourers. But
the Egyptian had no wish to continue the labours of
ploughing and reaping and preparing the ground for
the new crops in the world beyond the grave, therefore
he endeavoured to avoid this by getting the work done
vicariously. If words of power said over a figure could
make it to do evil, similarly words of power said over
a figure could make it to do good. At first a formula [1]
was composed, the recital of which was supposed to
relieve the deceased from the necessity of doing any
work whatsoever, and when the deceased himself had
said, " I lift up the hand of the man who is inactive.
" I have come from the city of Unnu (Hermopolis).
" I am the divine Soul which liveth, and I lead with
" me the hearts of the apes," his existence was thought
to be without toil. But, since the inhabitants of Sekhet-
Aaru needed food and drink, provision must be made
for their production, and the necessary labours of the
field must, in some manner, be performed. To meet
the difficulty a small stone figure of the deceased was
buried with him, but before it was laid in the tomb
the priests recited over it the words of power which
would cause it to do for the deceased whatever work
he might be adjudged to perform in the kingdom of
Osiris. Later, these words were inscribed upon the
figure in hieroglyphics, and later still the figure was

[1] *I.e.*, Chapter V. of the Book of the Dead.

provided with representations of the rope basket, and plough ⟨⟩, and flail ⟨⟩, such as were employed by the Egyptian labourer in carrying field produce, and in ploughing, and in threshing grain. The formula [1] or words of power which were inscribed on such figures varied at different periods, but one of the oldest, which was in use in the XVIIIth dynasty, makes the deceased say to the figure, which was called " Shabti " :—

" O thou Shabti figure of the scribe Nebseni, if I
" be called, or if I be adjudged to do any work what-
" soever of the labours which are to be done in the
" underworld by a man in his turn—behold, any
" obstacles (or opposition) to thee will be done away
" with there—let the judgment fall upon thee instead
" of upon me always, in the matter of sowing the fields,
" of filling the water-courses with water, and of bringing
" the sands from the east to the west." After these
words comes the answer by the figure, " Verily I am
" here, and [will do] whatsoever thou biddest me to
" do." The Egyptians were most anxious to escape
the labours of top-dressing [2] the land, and of sowing
the seed, a work which had to be done by a man
standing in water in the sun, and the toilsome task
of working the *shadûf*, or instrument for raising water

[1] *I.e.*, Chapter V. of the Book of the Dead.
[2] This is, I think, the meaning of bringing the sand from the east to the west.

from the Nile and turning it on to the land. In
graves not one figure only is found, but several, and
it is said that in the tomb of Seti I., king of Egypt
about B.C. 1370, no less than seven hundred wooden
ushabtiu inscribed with the VIth Chapter of the Book
of the Dead, and covered with bitumen, were found.
The use of the *shabti* figure continued unabated down
to the Roman period, when boxes full of ill-shaped,
uninscribed porcelain figures were buried in the tombs
with the dead.

The next instance worth mentioning of the use of
magical figures we obtain from the official account
of a conspiracy against Rameses III., king of Egypt
about B.C. 1200. It seems that a number of high
officials, the Overseer of the Treasury included, and
certain scribes, conspired together against this king,
apparently with the view of dethroning him. They
took into their counsels a number of the ladies attached
to the court (some think they belonged to the *harîm*),
and the chief abode of these ladies became the head-
quarters of the conspirators. One official was charged
with " carrying abroad their words to their mothers
"and sisters who were there to stir up men and to
" incite malefactors to do wrong to their lord "; another
was charged with aiding and abetting the conspiracy
by making himself one with the ringleaders; another
was charged with being cognizant of the whole matter,
and with concealing his knowledge of it; another with

"giving ear to the conversation held by the men con-
"spiring with the women of the Per-khent, and not
"bringing it forward against them," and so on. The
conspiracy soon extended from Egypt to Ethiopia, and
a military official of high rank in that country was
drawn into it by his sister, who urged him to " Incite
"the men to commit crime, and do thou thyself come
"to do wrong to thy lord"; now the sister of this
official was in the Per-khent, and so she was able to
give her brother the latest information of the progress
of the disaffection. Not content with endeavouring
to dethrone the king by an uprising of both soldiers
and civilians, Hui, a certain high official, who was
the overseer of the [royal] cattle, bethought him of
applying magic to help their evil designs, and with
this object in view he went to some one who had
access to the king's library, and he obtained from him
a book containing formulæ of a magical nature, and
directions for working magic. By means of this book
he obtained "divine power," and he became able to
cast spells upon folk. Having gained possession of
the book he next looked out for some place where he
could carry on his magical work without interruption,
and at length found one. Here he set to work to
make figures of men in wax, and amulets inscribed
with words of magical power which would provoke
love, and these he succeeded in introducing into the
royal palace by means of the official Athirmā; and

it seems as if those who took them into the palace
and those who received them were under the magical
influence of Hui. It is probable that the love philtres
were intended for the use of the ladies who were in-
volved in the conspiracy, but as to the object of the
wax figures there is no doubt, for they were intended
to work harm to the king. Meanwhile Hui studied
his magical work with great diligence, and he succeeded in finding efficacious means for carrying out
all the "horrible things and all the wickednesses
"which his heart could imagine"; these means he
employed in all seriousness, and at length committed
great crimes which were the horror of every god and
goddess, and the punishment of such crimes was death.
In another place Hui is accused of writing books or
formulæ of magical words, the effect of which would
be to drive men out of their senses, and to strike terror
into them; and of making gods of wax and figures of
men of the same substance, which should cause the
human beings whom they represented to become
paralysed and helpless. But their efforts were in
vain, the conspiracy was discovered, and the whole
matter was carefully investigated by two small courts
of enquiry, the members of which consisted, for the
most part, of the king's personal friends; the king's
orders to them were that "those who are guilty shall
"die by their own hands, and tell me nothing whatever
"about it." The first court, which consisted of six

members, sat to investigate the offences of the husbands
and relatives of the royal ladies, and those of the ladies
themselves, but before their business was done three
of them were arrested because it was found that the
ladies had gained great influence over them, that they
and the ladies had feasted together, and that they had
ceased to be, in consequence, impartial judges. They
were removed from their trusted positions before the
king, and having been examined and their guilt clearly
brought home to them, their ears and noses were cut
off as a punishment and warning to others not to form
friendships with the enemies of the king. The second
court, which consisted of five members, investigated
the cases of those who were charged with having
" stirred up men and incited malefactors to do wrong
" to their lord," and having found them guilty they
sentenced six of them to death, one by one, in the
following terms :—" Pentaura, who is also called by
" another name. He was brought up on account of the
" offence which he had committed in connexion with
" his mother Thi when she formed a conspiracy with
" the women of the Per-khent, and because he had
" intent to do evil unto his lord. He was brought
" before the court of judges that he might receive
" sentence, and they found him guilty, and dismissed
" him to his own death, where he suffered death by
" his own hand." The wretched man Hui, who made
wax figures and spells with the intent to inflict pain

and suffering and death upon the king, was also com-
pelled to commit suicide.[1]

The above story of the famous conspiracy against
Rameses III. is most useful as proving that books of
magic existed in the Royal Library, and that they were
not mere treatises on magical practices, but definite
works with detailed instructions to the reader how to
perform the ceremonies which were necessary to make
the formulæ or words of power efficacious. We have
now seen that wax figures were used both to do good
and to do harm, from the IIIrd to the XXth dynasty,
and that the ideas which the Egyptians held concerning
them were much the same about B.C. 1200 as they were
two thousand five hundred years earlier; we have also
seen that the use of *ushabtiu* figures, which were
intended to set the deceased free from the necessity of
labour in the world beyond the grave, was widespread.
That such figures were used in the pre-dynastic days
when the Egyptians were slowly emerging into civilization from a state of semi-barbarism is not to be
wondered at, and it need not surprise us that they
existed as a survival in the early dynasties before the
people generally had realized that the great powers of
Nature, which they deified, could not be ruled by man
and by his petty words and deeds, however mysterious
and solemn. It is, however, very remarkable to find

[1] See Devéria, *Le Papyrus Judiciaire de Turin* in *Journal Asiatique*,
1865; and Chabas, *Le Papyrus Magique Harris*, p. 169 ff.

G

that the use of wax figures played a prominent part in certain of the daily services which were performed in the temple of the god Amen-Rā at Thebes, and it is still more remarkable that these services were performed at a time when the Egyptians were renowned among the nations of the civilized world for their learning and wisdom. One ̍ company of priests attached to the temple was employed in transcribing hymns and religious compositions in which the unity, power, and might of God were set forth in unmistakable terms, and at the same time another company was engaged in performing a service the object of which was to free the Sun, which was deified under the form of Rā, and was the type and symbol of God upon earth, from the attacks of a monster called Āpep!

It will be remembered that the XXXIXth Chapter of the Book of the Dead is a composition which was written with the object of defeating a certain serpent, to which many names are given, and of delivering the deceased from his attacks. In it we have a description of how the monster is vanquished, and the deceased says to him, " Rā maketh thee to turn back, O thou " that art hateful to him ; he looketh upon thee, get " thee back. He pierceth thy head, he cutteth through " thy face, he divideth thy head at the two sides of the " ways, and it is crushed in his land ; thy bones are " smashed in pieces, thy members are hacked from off " thee, and the god Aker hath condemned thee, O Āpep,

" thou enemy of Rā. Get thee back, Fiend, before the
" darts of his beams! Rā hath overthrown thy words,
" the gods have turned thy face backwards, the Lynx
" hath torn open thy breast, the Scorpion hath cast
" fetters upon thee, and Maāt hath sent forth thy
" destruction. The gods of the south, and of the north,
" of the west, and of the east, have fastened chains upon
" him, and they have fettered him with fetters; the god
" Rekes hath overthrown him, and the god Hertit hath
" put him in chains." [1] The age of this composition is
unknown, but it is found, with variants, in many of the
copies of the Book of the Dead which were made in the
XVIIIth dynasty. Later, however, the ideas in it were
developed, the work itself was greatly enlarged, and at
the time of the Ptolemies it had become a book called
" The Book of Overthrowing Āpep," which contained
twelve chapters. At the same time another work
bearing the same title also existed; it was not divided
into chapters, but it contained two versions of the
history of the Creation, and a list of the evil names of
Āpep, and a hymn to Rā. [2] Among the chapters of the
former work was one entitled, " Chapter of putting the
" fire upon Āpep," which reads, " Fire be upon thee,
" Āpep, thou enemy of Rā! The Eye of Horus prevails
" over the accursed soul and shade of Āpep, and the

---

[1] See *Chapters of Coming Forth by Day*, p. 89.

[2] I have given a hieroglyphic transcript of both works, with translations, in *Archæologia*, Vol. LII.

" flame of the Eye of Horus shall gnaw into that enemy
" of Rā ; and the flame of the Eye of Horus shall con-
" sume all the enemies of the Mighty God, life !
" strength ! health ! both in death and in life. When
" Āpep is given to the flame," says the rubric, " thou
" shalt say these words of power :—Taste thou death,
" O Āpep, get thee back, retreat, O enemy of Rā, fall
" down, be repulsed, get back and retreat ! I have
" driven thee back, and I have cut thee in pieces.

" Rā triumphs over Āpep.　　Taste thou death, Āpep.
" Rā triumphs over Āpep.　　Taste thou death, Āpep.
" Rā triumphs over Āpep.　　Taste thou death, Āpep.
" Rā triumphs over Āpep.　　Taste thou death, Āpep."

These last sentences were said four times, that is to
say, once for each of the gods of the cardinal points.
The text continues, " Back, Fiend, an end to thee !
" Therefore have I driven flame at thee, and therefore
" have I made thee to be destroyed, and therefore have
" I adjudged thee to evil. An end, an end to thee !
" Taste thou death ! An end to thee ! Thou shalt never
" rise again." Such are the words of power, and these
are followed by the directions for performing the
ceremony, which read thus :—

" If thou wouldst destroy Āpep, thou shalt say this
" chapter over a figure of Āpep which hath been drawn
" in green colour upon a sheet of new papyrus, and over

" a wax figure [1] of Āpep upon which his name hath been
" cut and inlaid with green colour; and thou shalt lay
" them upon the fire so that it may consume the enemy
" of Rā. And thou shalt put such a figure on the fire
" at dawn, and another at noon, and another at even-
" tide when Rā setteth in the land of life, and another
" at midnight, and another at the eighth hour of the
" day, and another towards evening; [and if necessary]
" thou mayest do thus every hour during the day and
" the night, and on the days of the festivals . . . and
" every day. By means of this Āpep, the enemy of Rā,
" shall be overthrown in the shower, for Rā shall shine
" and Āpep shall indeed be overthrown." And the
papyrus and the figure " having been burnt in a fire
" made of *khesau* grass, the remains thereof shall be
" mixed with excrement and thrown upon a fire; thou
" shalt do this at the sixth hour of the night, and at
" dawn on the fifteenth day [of the month]. And
" when the figure of Āpep is placed in the fire thou
" shalt spit upon him several times each hour during
" the day, until the shadow turneth round. Thou shalt
" do these things when tempests rage in the east of the
" sky as Rā setteth, in order to prevent the coming
" onward of the storms. Thou shalt do this and so

---

[1] Theocritus has preserved for us a proof that the Greeks made use
of wax figures at an early date. Thus in *Pharmakeutria* (l. 27 ff.) the
lady spinning her wheel and addressing the Lynx says, " Even as I
" melt this wax, with the god to aid, so speedily may he by love be
" molten ! " (Lang's *Translation*, p. 12).

"prevent the coming of a shower or a rain-storm, and
"thereby shall the sun be made to shine."

In another part of this book the reciter is told to
say the following "firmly with the mouth" :—"Down
"upon thy face, O Āpep, enemy of Rā! The flame
"which cometh forth from the Eye of Horus advanceth
"against thee. Thou art thrust down into the flame
"of fire and it cometh against thee. Its flame is deadly
"to thy soul, and to thy spirit, and to thy words of
"power, and to thy body, and to thy shade. The lady
"of fire prevaileth over thee, the flame pierceth thy
"soul, it maketh an end of thy person, and it darteth
"into thy form. The eye of Horus which is powerful
"against its enemy hath cast thee down, it devoureth
"thee, the great fire trieth thee, the Eye of Rā prevaileth
"over thee, the flame devoureth thee, and what escapeth
"from it hath no being. Get thee back, for thou art
"cut asunder, thy soul is shrivelled up, thy accursed
"name is buried in oblivion, and silence is upon it,
"and it hath fallen [out of remembrance]. Thou hast
"come to an end, thou hast been driven away, and
"thou art forgotten, forgotten, forgotten," etc. To
make these words to be of effect the speaker is told
to write the names of Āpep upon a new papyrus and
to burn it in the fire either when Rā is rising, or at
noon, or at sunset, etc. In another part of the work,
after a series of curses which are ordered to be said
over Āpep, the rubric directs that they shall be recited

by a person who hath washed himself and is ceremonially clean, and when this has been done he is to write
in green colour upon a piece of new papyrus the names
of all the fiends who are in the train of Āpep, as well
as those of their fathers, and mothers, and children.
He must then make figures of all these fiends in wax,
and having inscribed their names upon them, must tie
them up with black hair, and then cast them on the
ground and kick them with the left foot, and pierce
them with a stone spear; this done they are to be
thrown into the fire. More than once is it said, " It
" is good for a man to recite this book before the august
" god regularly," for the doing of it was believed to
give great power " to him, both upon earth and in the
" underworld." Finally, after the names of Āpep are
enumerated, he who would benefit by the knowledge
of them is bidden to " make the figure of a serpent
" with his tail in his mouth, and having stuck a knife
" in his back, cast him down upon the ground and say,
" ' Āpep, Fiend, Betet.' " Then, in order to destroy
the fiends who are in the train of Āpep, other images
or figures of them must be made with their hands tied
behind them; these are to be called " Children of
" inactivity." The papyrus then continues, " Make
" another serpent with the face of a cat, and with a
" knife stuck in his back, and call it ' Hemhem '
" (Roarer). Make another with the face of a croco-
" dile, and with a knife stuck in his back, and call it

" ' Hauna-aru-her-hra.'   Make another with the face of
" a duck, and with a knife stuck in his back, and call it
" ' Aluti.' Make another with the face of a white cat, and
" with a knife stuck in his back, and tie it up and bind
" it tightly, and call it 'Āpep the Enemy.' "   Such are
the means which the Egyptians adopted when they
wanted to keep away rain and storm, thunder and
lightning, and mist and cloud, and to ensure a bright
clear sky wherein the sun might run his course.

Under the heading of " Magical Figures " must
certainly be included the so-called Ptah-Seker-Ausar
figure which is usually made of wood; it is often
solid, but is sometimes made hollow, and is usually
let into a rectangular wooden stand which may be
either solid or hollow. The three gods or trinity of
Ptah, Seker (Socharis), and Ausar (Osiris), are intended
to represent the god of the sunrise (Ptah), the god
of the night sun (Seker), and the god of the resurrection
(Osiris). The name Ptah means " Opener," and is
usually applied to the sun as the " opener " of the
day; and the name Seker means " He who is shut in,"
that is to say, the night sun, who was regarded as the
sun buried temporarily. Now the life of a man upon
earth was identified with that of the sun; he " opened "
or began his life as Ptah, and after death he was " shut
" in " or " coffined," like it also. But the sun rises again
when the night is past, and, as it begins a new life
with renewed strength and vigour, it became the type

of the new life which the Egyptian hoped to live in
the world beyond the grave. But the difficulty was
how to obtain the protection of Ptah, Seker, and Osiris,
and how to make them do for the man that which
they did for themselves, and so secure their attributes.
To attain this end a figure was fashioned in such a
way as to include the chief characteristics of the forms
of these gods, and was inserted in a rectangular wooden
stand which was intended to represent the coffin or
chest out of which the trinity Ptah-Seker-Ausar came
forth.   On the figure itself and on the sides of the
stand were inscribed prayers on behalf of the man for
whom it was made, and the Egyptian believed that
these prayers caused the might and powers of the three
gods to come and dwell in the wooden figure. But
in order to make the stand of the figure as much like
a coffin as possible, a small portion of the body of the
deceased was carefully mummified and placed in it,
and it was thought that if the three gods protected
and preserved that piece, and if they revivified it in
due season, the whole body would be protected, and
preserved, and revivified. Frequently, especially in
the late period, a cavity was made in the side of the
stand, and in this was laid a small roll of papyrus
inscribed with the text of certain Chapters of the Book
of the Dead, and thus the deceased was provided with
additional security for the resurrection of his spiritual
body in the world to come. The little rolls of papyrus

are often inscribed with but short and fragmentary texts, but occasionally, as in the case of the priestess Anhai, a fine large papyrus,[1] inscribed with numerous texts and illustrated with vignettes, was placed inside the figure of the god, who in this instance is in the form of Osiris only.[2] It seems that the Ptah-Seker-Ausar figure was much used in the late period in Egypt, for many inscribed examples have been found which are not only illegible, but which prove that the artist had not the remotest idea of the meaning of the things which he was writing. It is possible that they were employed largely by the poor, among whom they seem to have served the purpose of the costly tomb.

Returning once more to the subject of wax figures, it may be wondered why such a very large proportion of the figures of the gods which were worn by the living and attached to the bodies of the dead as amulets are made of almost every kind of substance except wax. But the reason of this is not far to seek: wax is a substance which readily changes its form under heat and pressure, and it is also possible that the fact of its having been employed from time immemorial for making figures which were intended to work harm and not good to man, induced those who made amulets in the forms of the gods to select some other material. As a matter of fact, however, several figures of gods

---

[1] This papyrus is preserved in the British Museum (No. 10,472).
[2] British Museum, No. 20,868.

Ptah-Seker-Ausar figure with cavity containing a portion of a human body mummified.
(British Museum, No. 9736.)

made of wax to serve as protective amulets are known, and a set of four, representing the four children of Horus, now preserved in the British Museum, are worthy of notice. The four children of Horus, or the gods of the four cardinal points, were called Mestha, Hāpi, Tuamutef, and Qebhsennuf, and with them were associated the goddesses Isis, Nephthys, Neith, and Serqet respectively. Mestha was man-headed, and represented the south, and protected the stomach and large intestines; Hāpi was dog-headed, and represented the north, and protected the small intestines; Tuamutef was jackal-headed, and represented the east, and protected the lungs and the heart; and Qebhsennuf was hawk-headed, and represented the west, and protected the liver and the gall-bladder. The various internal organs of men were removed from the body before it was mummified, and having been steeped in certain astringent substances and bitumen were wrapped up in bandages, and laid in four jars made of stone, marble, porcelain, earthenware, or wood. Each jar was placed under the protection of one of the four children of Horus, and as it was hollow, and its cover was made in the form of the head of the god who was represented by it, and as the jar by means of the inscription upon it became an abode of the god, it might well be said that the organ of the deceased which was put in it was actually placed inside the god. The custom of embalming the intestines separately is very old, and several examples of it in the XIth dynasty are known ; even at that early period the four jars of mummified intestines were placed in a funeral chest, or coffer, which was mounted on a sledge, and drawn along in the funeral procession immediately after the coffin. In later times we find that many attempts were made to secure for the deceased the benefit of the protection of these four gods without incurring the expense of

The Four Children of Horus.

Hāpi.   Mestha.   Tuamutef. Qebhsennuf.

Osiris rising from the funeral chest holding the symbol of "life" in each hand.
(From the *Papyrus of Ani*, plate 8.)

stone jars ; this could be done by burying with him four models or " dummy " jars, or four porcelain figures of the four gods, 𓀀, 𓀀, 𓀀, 𓀀, or four wax ones. For some unknown reason the set referred to above was made of wax.[1] The four children of Horus played a

[1] Nos. 15,563, 15,564, 15,573, and 15,578 in the Second Egyptian Room.

very important part in the funeral works of the early
dynasties; they originally represented the four sup-
ports of heaven, but very soon each was regarded as
the god of one of the four quarters of the earth, and
also of that quarter of the heavens which was above
it. As the constant prayer of the deceased was that
he should be able to go about wherever he pleased,
both on earth and in heaven, it was absolutely necessary for his welfare that he should propitiate these
gods and place himself under their protection, which
could only be secured by the recital of certain words
of power over figures of them, or over jars made to
represent them.

But of all the Egyptians who were skilled in working magic, Nectanebus, the last native king of Egypt,
about B.C. 358, was the chief, if we may believe Greek
tradition. According to Pseudo-Callisthenes, and the
versions of his works which were translated into Pehlevi,
Arabic, Syriac, and a score of other languages and
dialects, this king was famous as a magician and a
sage, and he was deeply learned in all the wisdom of
the Egyptians. He knew what was in the depths
of the Nile and of heaven, he was skilled in reading
the stars, in interpreting omens, in casting nativities,
in telling fortunes, and in predicting the future of the
unborn child, and in working magic of every kind, as
we shall see; he was said to be the lord of the earth,
and to rule all kings by means of his magical powers.

Whenever he was threatened with invasion by sea or
by land he succeeded in destroying the power of his
enemies, and in driving them from his coasts or
frontiers; and this he did by the following means.
If the enemy came against him by sea, instead of
sending out his sailors to fight them, he retired into
a certain chamber, and having brought forth a bowl
which he kept for the purpose, he filled it with water,
and then, having made wax figures of the ships and
men of the enemy, and also of his own men and ships,
he set them upon the water in the bowl, his men on
one side, and those of the enemy on the other. He
then came out, and having put on the cloak of an
Egyptian prophet and taken an ebony rod in his hand,
he returned into the chamber, and uttering words of
power he invoked the gods who help men to work
magic, and the winds, and the subterranean demons,
which straightway came to his aid. By their means
the figures of the men in wax sprang into life and
began to fight, and the ships of wax began to move
about likewise; but the figures which represented his
own men vanquished those which represented the
enemy, and as the figures of the ships and men of the
hostile fleet sank through the water to the bottom of the
bowl, even so did the real ships and men sink through
the waters to the bottom of the sea. In this way he
succeeded in maintaining his power, and he continued
to occupy his kingdom in peace for a considerable

period. But it fell out on a day that certain scouts
came and informed Nectanebus that a multitude of
the nations of the East had made a league together
against Egypt, and that their allied forces were at that
moment marching against him. When the king heard
the news he laughed, and having said some scornful
words about his enemies, he went into his private
chamber, and pouring water into the bowl began to
work magic in the usual way. But when he had
spoken the words of power, he looked at the wax
figures, and saw, to his dismay, that the gods of Egypt
were steering the enemies' ships, and leading their
soldiers to war against himself. Now as soon as
Nectanebus saw this, he understood that the end of
the kingdom of Egypt was at hand, for hitherto the
gods had been wont to hold converse with him readily,
and to lend him their help whenever he had need of
it. He then quitted the chamber hastily, and having
shaved off his hair and his beard, and disguised
himself by putting on common apparel, he took
ship and fled to Pella in Macedonia, where he established himself as a physician, and as an Egyptian
soothsayer.

Omitting, for the present, any reference to the con-
tents of the IVth chapter of Pseudo-Callisthenes, in
which the casting of the nativity of Olympias by
Nectanebus is described, we come to the passage in
which the story of the way in which he sent a dream

H

to the queen by means of a wax figure is told. His
object was to persuade the queen that the Egyptian
god Amen would come to her at night. To do this
he left her presence, and going out into the desert he
collected a number of herbs which he knew how to
employ in causing people to dream dreams, and having
brought them back with him he squeezed the juice
out of them. He then made the figure of a woman
in wax, and wrote upon it the name of Olympias, just
as the priest of Thebes made the figure of Āpep in
wax and cut his name upon it. Nectanebus then lit
his lamp, and, having poured the juice of the herbs
over the wax figure of the queen, he adjured the
demons to such purpose that Olympias dreamed a
dream in which the god Amen came to her and
embraced her, and told her that she should give birth
to a man-child who should avenge her on her husband
Philip. But the means described above were not the
only ones known to Nectanebus for procuring dreams,
for when he wanted to make Philip of Macedon to
see certain things in a dream, and to take a certain
view about what he saw, he sent a hawk, which he
had previously bewitched by magical words, to Philip
as he lay asleep, and in a single night the hawk flew
from Macedonia to the place where Philip was, and
coming to him told him what things he should see
in his dream, and he saw them. On the morrow Philip
had the dream explained by an expounder of dreams,

and he was satisfied that the child[1] to whom his wife
Olympias was about to give birth was the son of the
god Amen (or Ammon) of Libya, who was regarded
as the father of all the kings who ascended the throne
of Egypt, who did not belong to the royal stock of
that country.[2]

Here, in connexion with the Egyptian use of wax
figures, must be mentioned one or two stories and
traditions of Alexander the Great which are, clearly,
derived from Egyptian sources.   The Arab writer,
Abu-Shâker, who flourished in the XIIIth century of
our era, mentions a tradition that Aristotle gave to
Alexander a number of wax figures nailed down in
a box, which was fastened by a chain, and which he
ordered him never to let go out of his hand, or at least
out of that of one of his confidential servants.   The
box was to go wherever Alexander went, and Aristotle
taught him to recite certain formulæ over it whenever
he took it up or put it down.   The figures in the box
were intended to represent the various kinds of armed
forces that Alexander was likely to find opposed to
him.   Some of the models held in their hands leaden
swords which were curved backwards, and some had
spears in their hands pointed head downwards, and
some had bows with cut strings ; all these were laid
face downwards in the box.   Viewed by what we

[1] *I.e.*, Alexander the Great.
[2] For further mention of dreams, see the last chapter in this book.

know of the ideas which underlay the use of wax figures by the Egyptians and Greeks, it is clear that, in providing Alexander with these models and the words of power to use with them, Aristotle believed he was giving him the means of making his enemies to become like the figures in the box, and so they would be powerless to attack him.[1]

In the Græco-Roman period[2] wax figures were used in the performance of magical ceremonies of every kind, and the two following examples indicate that the ideas which underlay their use had not changed in the least. If a lover wished to secure the favours of his mistress, he is directed to make a figure of a dog in wax mixed with pitch, gum, etc., eight fingers long, and certain words of power are to be written over the place where his ribs should be. Next it was necessary to write on a tablet other words of power, or the names of beings who were supposed to possess magical powers ; on this tablet the figure of the dog must be placed, and the tablet is made to rest upon a tripod. When this has been done the lover must recite the words of power which are written on the dog's side, and also the names which have been inscribed on the tablet, and one of two things will happen : *i.e.*, the dog will either snarl

[1] See my *Life and Exploits of Alexander the Great* (one volume edition), p. xvi.

[2] The Greeks used incantations at an early date, as we may see from Pindar, *Pythia*, iv. 213 ; this writer lived in the first half of the fifth century before Christ.

and snap at the lover, or he will bark. If he snarls and snaps the lover will not gain the object of his affections, but if he barks the lady will come to him. In the second example the lover is ordered to make two waxen figures; one in the form of Ares, and the other in the form of a woman. The female figure is to be in the posture of kneeling upon her knees with her hands tied behind her, and the male figure is to stand over her with his sword at her throat. On the limbs of the female figure a large number of the names of demons are to be written, and when this has been done, the lover must take thirteen bronze needles, and stick them in her limbs, saying as he does so, "I pierce" (here he mentions the name of the limb) "that she may think of "me." The lover must next write certain words of power on a leaden plate, which must be tied to the wax figures with a string containing three hundred and sixty-five knots, and both figure and plate are to be buried in the grave of some one who has died young or who has been slain by violence. He must then recite a long incantation to the infernal gods, and if all these things be done in a proper manner the lover will obtain the woman's affections.[1]

From Egypt, by way of Greece and Rome, the use of

[1] I owe the facts of these two examples of the use of wax figures and the two spells for procuring visions and dreams (see p. 96), and the example of the use of the sphere of Democritus (p. 230), to Mr. F. G. Kenyon, Assistant Keeper in the Dept. of MSS., British Museum.

wax figures passed into Western Europe and England, and in the Middle Ages it found great favour with those who interested themselves in the working of the "black "art," or who wished to do their neighbour or enemy an injury. Many stories are current of how in Italy and England ignorant or wicked-minded people made models of their enemies in wax and hung them up in the chimney, not too close to the fire, so that they might melt away slowly, and of how the people that were represented by such figures gradually lost the power over their limbs, and could not sleep, and slowly sickened and died.   If pins and needles were stuck into the wax figures at stated times the sufferings of the living were made more agonizing, and their death much more painful.

Sharpe relates[1] that about the end of the VIIth century king Duffus was so unpopular that " a company " of hags roasted his image made of wax upon a wooden " spit, reciting certain words of enchantment, and basting " the figure with a poisonous liquor. These women when " apprehended declared that as the wax melted, the body " of the king should decay, and the words of enchant- " ment prevented him from the refreshment of sleep." The two following extracts from Thomas Middleton's *The Witch* [2] illustrate the views held about wax figures in England in the time of this writer.[3]

---

[1] See C. K. Sharpe, *Witchcraft in Scotland*, London, 1884, p. 21.
[2] London, 1778.   [3] Born about 1570, died about 1626.

I.

" *Heccat.* Is the heart of wax
        Stuck full of magique needles ?
" *Stadlin.* 'Tis done Heccat.
" *Heccat.* And is the Farmer's picture, and his wives,
        Lay'd downe to th' fire yet ?
" *Stadlin.* They are a roasting both too.
" *Heccat.* Good :
        Then their marrowes are a melting subtelly
        And three monethes sicknes sucks up life in
        'em."

(Act i., scene 2.)

II.

" *Heccat.* What death is't you desire for Almachildes ?
" *Duchesse.* A sodaine and a subtle.
" *Heccat.* Then I have fitted you.
        Here lye the guifts of both ; sodaine and
        subtle :
        His picture made in wax, and gently molten
        By a blew fire kindled with dead mens' eyes
        Will waste him by degrees."

(Act v., scene 2.)

Mr. Elworthy in his very interesting book "The
" Evil Eye "[1] relates some striking examples of the burning of hearts stuck full of pins for magical purposes

[1] London, 1895, pp. 53, 56.

in recent years. Thus an old woman at Mendip had
a pig that fell ill, and she at once made up her mind
that the animal had been "overlooked"; in her trouble
she consulted a "white witch," *i.e.* a "wise" man, and
by his orders she acted thus. She obtained a sheep's
heart, and having stuck it full of pins [1] set it to roast
before a fire, whilst her friends and neighbours sang:—

> "It is not this heart I mean to burn,
> But the person's heart I wish to turn,
> Wishing them neither rest nor peace
> Till they are dead and gone."

At intervals her son George sprinkled salt on the fire
which added greatly to the weirdness of the scene, and
at length, when the roasting had been continued until
far into the night, a black cat jumped out from some-
where and was, of course, instantly declared to be the
demon which had been exorcised. Again, in October,
1882, a heart stuck full of pins was found in a recess
of a chimney in an old house in the village of Ash-
brittle; and in 1890 another was found nailed up inside
the "clavel" in the chimney of an old house at Staple-
grove.

The art of making such figures King James I.
attributes to the "Divell," and says in describing the

---

[1] In the North Riding of Yorkshire evil influences were averted
by means of a living black cock which "was pierced with pins and
"roasted alive at dead of night, with every door, window, and cranny
"and crevice stuffed up" (see Blakeborough, *Wit, Character, Folk-lore
and Customs of the North Riding of Yorkshire*, London, 1898, p. 205).

things which witches are able to " effectuate by the
" power of their master[1] " :—" To some others at these
"times hee teacheth, how to make pictures of waxe
" or clay : That by the roasting thereof, the persons
" that they beare the name of, may be continually
" melted or dried away by continuall sicknesse. . . .
" They can bewitch and take the life of men or women,
" by roasting of the pictures, as I spake of before, which
" likewise is verie possible to their Maister to performe,
" for although (as I said before) that instrument of waxe
" have no vertue in that turne doing, yet may hee not
" very well, even by the same measure that his conjured
" slaves, melts that waxe at the fire, may hee not, I say
" at these same times, subtily, as a sp:rite, so weaken
" and scatter the spirites of life of the patient, as may
" make him on the one part, for faintnesse, so sweate
" out the humour of his bodie : And on the other parte,
" for the not concurrence of these spirites, which causes
" his digestion, so debilitate his stomacke, that this
" humour radicall continually sweating out on the one
" part, and no new good sucke being put in the place
" thereof, for lacke of digestion on the other, he at last
" shall vanish away, even as his picture will die at the
" fire ?   And that knavish and cunning workeman, by
" troubling him, onely at sometimes, makes a proportion,
" so neere betwixt the working of the one and the other,

[1] The following words are put into the mouth of Epistemon in
Dæmonologie, in Forme of ane Dialogue, London, 1603, Second Booke,
Chap. V. pp. 44. 45.

" that both shall end as it were at one time." Thus we
have seen that the belief in the efficacy of wax figures
is at least six thousand years old, and judging from
passages in the works of modern writers its existence is
not unknown in our own country at the present time.

This chapter may be fittingly ended by a notice of
the benefits which accrued to a Christian merchant in
the Levant from the use of a wax figure. According to
an Ethiopic manuscript in the British Museum[1] this
man was a shipowner as well as a merchant, and he
was wont to send his goods to market in his own ships;
in his day, however, the sea was infested with pirates,
and he lost greatly through their successful attacks
upon his vessels. At length he determined to travel in
one of his own ships with a number of armed men, so
that he might be able to resist any attack which the
pirates might make, and punish them for their robberies
in times past. Soon after he had sailed he fell in with
a pirate vessel, and a fight at once took place between
his crew and the robbers, in the course of which he
was shot in the eye by an arrow; he stopped the
combat and then sailed for a port which was situated
near a monastery, wherein the Virgin Mary was reported to work miracles by means of a picture of herself
which was hung up in it. When the merchant arrived
in port he was so ill through the wound in his eye that
he could not be moved, and it was found that a portion

[1] Oriental 646, fol. 29*b* ff.

of the arrow which had struck him remained embedded
in it; and unless he could obtain the Virgin's help
speedily he felt that his death was nigh. In this
difficulty a certain Christian came to the ship and
made a wax figure of the merchant, and, having stuck
in one eye a model of the arrow which had struck him,
carried the figure to the monastery, which was some
miles off, and caused the monks to allow him to bring
it nigh to the picture of the Virgin. When this had
been done, and prayers had been made to her, the
figure of the Virgin stretched out its hand, and straightway pulled the model of the arrow out of the eye of
the wax figure of the merchant in such a way that no
broken fragment remained behind. When the wax
figure had been taken back to the ship, it was found
that the piece of broken arrow had been extracted from
the merchant's eye at the very moment when the
Virgin had drawn out the arrow from the eye of the
wax figure. The merchant's eye then healed, and he
recovered his sight.

CHAPTER IV.

FROM what has been said above it is clear that the
Egyptian believed it possible to vivify by means of
formulæ and words of power any figure made in the
form of a man or animal, and to make it work either
on behalf of or against his fellow man. Besides this,
he believed greatly in the efficacy of representations or
pictures of the gods, and of divine beings and things,
provided that words of power properly recited by
properly appointed people were recited over them. If
this fact be borne in mind a great many difficulties in
understanding religious texts disappear, and many
apparently childish facts are seen to have an important
meaning. If we look into the tombs of the early
period we see painted on the walls numbers of scenes
in which the deceased is represented making offerings
to the gods and performing religious ceremonies, as
well as numbers of others in which he is directing the
work of his estate and ruling his household. It was
not altogether the result of pride that such pictures

were painted on the walls of tombs, for at the bottom of his heart the Egyptian hoped and believed that they were in reality representations of what he would do in the next world, and he trusted that the words of his prayers would turn pictures into realities, and drawings into substances. The wealthy Egyptian left behind him the means for making the offerings which his *ka*,

The goddess Hathor giving the scribe Ani meat and drink from out of a sycamore tree which grows by the side of a stream.   (From the *Papyrus of Ani*, plate 16.)

or double, needed, and was able to provide for the maintenance of his tomb and of the *ka* chapel and of the priest or priests who ministered to it.   It was an article of faith among all classes that unless the *ka* was properly fed it would be driven to wander about and pick up filth and anything else of that nature which it

found in its path, as we may see from the LIInd
Chapter of the Book of the Dead, in which the deceased
says, "That which is an abomination unto me, that
"which is an abomination unto me let me not eat.
" That which is an abomination unto me, that which is
"an abomination unto me is filth; let me not eat of it
"instead of the cakes [which are offered unto] the
"Doubles (*kau*). Let it not light upon my body; let
"me not be obliged to take it into my hands; and let

The scribe Ani and his wife standing in a stream drinking water.
(From the *Papyrus of Ani*, plate 16.)

"me not be obliged to walk thereon in my sandals."
And in the CLXXXIXth Chapter he prays that he
may not be obliged to drink filthy water or be de-
filed in any way by it. The rich man, even, was not
certain that the appointed offerings of meat and drink
could or would be made in his tomb in perpetuity:
what then was the poor man to do to save his *ka* from
the ignominy of eating filth and drinking dirty water ?

To get out of this difficulty the model of an altar in stone was made, and models of cakes, vases of water, fruit, meat, etc., were placed upon it; in cases where this was not possible figures of the offerings were sculptured upon the stone itself; in others, where even the expense of an altar could not be borne by the relatives of the dead, an altar with offerings painted upon it was placed in the tomb, and as long as it existed through the prayers recited, the *ka* did not lack food. Sometimes neither altar, nor model nor picture of an altar was placed in the tomb, and the prayer that sepulchral meals might be given to the deceased by the gods, which was inscribed upon some article of funeral furniture, was the only provision made for the wants of the *ka;* but every time any one who passed by the tomb recited that prayer, and coupled with it the name of the man who was buried in it, his *ka* was provided with a fresh supply of meat and drink offerings, for the models or pictures of them in the inscription straight-way became veritable substances. On the insides of the wooden coffins of the XIIth dynasty, about B.C. 2500, are painted whole series of objects which, in still earlier times, were actually placed in the tombs with the mummy; but little by little men ceased to provide the numerous articles connected with the sepulture of the dead which the old ritual prescribed, and they trusted to the texts and formulæ which they painted on the coffin to turn pictures into substances, and besides the pillow they placed little else in the tomb.

About a thousand years later, when the religious texts which formed the Book of the Dead were written upon papyri instead of coffins, a large number of illustrations or vignettes were added to them ; to many of these special importance was attached, and the following are worthy of note.

It will be remembered that the CXXVth Chapter of the Book of the Dead contains the so-called " Negative Confession " which is recited in the Hall of Maāti, and a number of names of gods and beings, the knowledge of which is most important for the welfare of the deceased. At the end of the Chapter we find the following statement :—" This chapter shall be said by " the deceased after he hath been cleansed and purified, " and when he is arrayed in apparel, and is shod with " white leather sandals, and his eyes have been painted " with antimony, and his body hath been anointed with " *anti* unguent, and when he hath made offerings of " oxen, and birds, and incense, and cakes, and ale, and " garden herbs. And behold, thou shalt paint a picture " of what shall happen in the Hall of Maāti upon a " new tile moulded from earth, upon which neither a " pig nor any other animal hath trodden. And if thou " writest upon it this chapter the deceased shall " flourish ; and his children shall flourish ; and his " name shall never fall into oblivion ; and bread, and

"cakes, and sweetmeats, and wine, and meat shall be
"given unto him at the altar of the great god; and he
"shall not be turned back at any door in the under-
"world; and he shall be brought in along with the
"Kings of the North and South; and he shall be in
"the following of Osiris always and for ever." Here,
then, we have an excellent example of the far-reaching
effects of a picture accompanied by the proper words of
power, and every picture in the Book of the Dead was
equally efficacious in producing a certain result, that result being always connected with the welfare of the dead.

According to several passages and chapters the
deceased was terrified lest he should lack both air and
water, as well as food, in the underworld, and, to do
away with all risk of such a calamity happening,
pictures, in which he is represented holding a sail (the
symbol of air and wind and breath) in his hands, and
standing up to his ankles in water,[1] were painted on
his papyrus, and texts similar to the following were
written below them. "My mouth and my nostrils are
"opened in Tattu (Busiris), and I have my place of
"peace in Annu (Heliopolis) which is my house; it
"was built for me by the goddess Sesheta, and the god
"Khnemu set it upon its walls for me. . . ." "Hail,
"thou god Tem, grant thou unto me the sweet breath
"which dwelleth in thy nostrils! I embrace the great
"throne which is in Khemennu (Hermopolis), and I

[1] See the vignettes to Chapters LIV.-LX. of the Book of the Dead.

I

"keep watch over the Egg of the Great Cackler; I
" germinate as it germinateth; I live as it liveth; and
" my breath is its breath."[1]   But yet another " exceed-
"ingly great mystery" had to be performed if the
deceased was to be enabled to enter into heaven by its
four doors at will,. and to enjoy the air which came
through each.   The north wind belonged to Osiris, the
south wind to Rā, the west wind to Isis, and the east
wind to Nephthys; and for the deceased to obtain
power over each and all of these it was necessary for
him to be master of the doors through which they blew.
This power could only be obtained by causing pictures
of the four doors to be painted on the coffin with a
figure of Thoth opening each.   Some special importance
was attached to these, for the rubric says, " Let none
" who is outside know this chapter, for it is a great
" mystery, and those who dwell in the swamps (i.e., the
"ignorant) know it not.   Thou shalt not do this in the
"presence of any person except thy father, or thy son,
" or thyself alone; for it is indeed an exceedingly great
"mystery which no man whatever knoweth." [2]

One of the delights coveted by the deceased was to
sail over heaven in the boat of Rā, in company with
the gods of the funeral cycle of Osiris; this happiness
could be secured for him by painting certain pictures,
and by saying over them certain words of power.   On

[1] See *Chapters of Coming Forth by Day*, p. 106.
[2] *Ibid.*, p. 289.

a piece of clean papyrus a boat is to be drawn with ink made of green *ābut* mixed with *ānti* water, and in it are to be figures of Isis, Thoth, Shu, and Khepera, and the deceased; when this has been done the papyrus must be fastened to the breast of the deceased, care being taken that it does not actually touch his body. Then shall his spirit enter into the boat of Rā each day, and the god Thoth shall take heed to him, and he shall sail about with Rā into any place that he wisheth.[1] Elsewhere it is ordered that the boat of Rā be painted "in a pure place," and in the bows is to be painted a figure of the deceased; but Rā was supposed to travel in one boat (called "Ātet ") until noon, and another (called "Sektet ") until sunset, and provision had to be made for the deceased in both boats. How was this to be done? On one side of the picture of the boat a figure of the morning boat of Rā was to be drawn, and on the other a figure of the afternoon boat; thus the one picture was capable of becoming two boats. And, provided the proper offerings were made for the deceased on the birthday of Osiris, his soul would live for ever, and he would not die a second time.[2] According to the rubric to the chapter [3] in which these directions are given, the text of it is as old, at least, as the time of Hesepti, the fifth king of the Ist dynasty, who reigned about B.C. 4350, and the custom of painting the boat upon

---

[1] See *Chapters of Coming Forth by Day*, p. 162.
[2] *Ibid.*, p. 212.   [3] *I.e.*, CXXX.

papyrus is probably contemporaneous. The two following rubrics from Chapters CXXXIII. and CXXXIV.,
respectively, will explain still further the importance of
such pictures :—

1. "This chapter shall be recited over a boat four
"cubits in length, and made of green porcelain [on
"which have been painted] the divine sovereign chiefs
"of the cities; and a figure of heaven with its stars
"shall be made also, and this thou shalt have made
"ceremonially pure by means of natron and incense.
"And behold, thou shalt make an image of Rā in
"yellow colour upon a new plaque and set it at the
"bows of the boat. And behold, thou shalt make an
"image of the spirit which thou dost wish to make
"perfect [and place it] in this boat, and thou shalt
"make it to travel about in the boat [which shall be
"made in the form of the boat] of Rā; and he shall
"see the form of the god Rā himself therein. Let not
"the eye of any man whatsoever look upon it, with the
"exception of thine own self, or thy father, or thy son,
"and guard [this] with great care. Then shall the
"spirit be perfect in the heart of Rā, and it shall give
"unto him power with the company of the gods; and
"the gods shall look upon him as a divine being like
"unto themselves; and mankind and the dead shall
"fall down upon their faces, and he shall be seen in
"the underworld in the form of the radiance of Rā."

2. "This chapter shall be recited over a hawk

" standing and having the white crown upon his head,
" [and over figures of] the gods Tem, Shu, Tefnut, Seb,
" Nut, Osiris, Isis, Suti, and Nephthys, painted in yellow
" colour upon a new plaque, which shall be placed in
" [a model of] the boat [of Rā], along with a figure of
" the spirit whom thou wouldst make perfect.   These
" thou shalt anoint with cedar oil, and incense shall be
" offered up to them on the fire, and feathered fowl,

The soul of the scribe Ani visiting his mummified body as it lies on its bier in the
tomb.   (From the *Papyrus of Ani*, plate 17.)

" shall be roasted.   It is an act of praise to Rā as he
" journeyeth, and it shall cause a man to have his being
" along with Rā day by day, whithersoever the god
" voyageth ; and it shall destroy the enemies of Rā in
" very truth regularly and continually."

Many of the pictures or vignettes carry their own
interpretations with them, *e.g.*, the picture of the soul
hovering over the dead body which lies beneath it on
the bier at once suggests the reunion of the soul with

the body; the picture of the deceased walking away
from a "block of slaughter" and a knife dripping with
blood suggests escape from a cruel death; the picture
of a soul and spirit standing before an open door
suggests that the soul has freedom to wander about at
will; and the picture of the soul and the shadow in
the act of passing out through the door of the tomb
indicates clearly that these parts of man's economy are

Anubis holding the mummy of the scribe Ani; by the door of the tomb stand the
soul and spirit of the deceased in the form of a human-headed hawk and *bennu*
bird respectively. (From the *Papyrus of Ani*, plate 16.)

not shut up in the tomb for all eternity. But the ideas
which prompted the painting of other vignettes are
not so clear, *e.g.*, those which accompany Chapters
CLXII.–CLXV. in the late or Säite Recension of the
Book of the Dead, although, fortunately, the rubrics to
these chapters make their object clear. Thus the picture
which stands above Chapter CLXII. is that of a cow
having upon her head horns, a disk, and two plumes,

and from the rubric we learn that a figure of it was to
be made in gold and fastened to the neck of the
deceased, and that another, drawn upon new papyrus,
was to be placed under his head. If this be done
"then shall abundant warmth be in him throughout,
"even like that which was in him when he was upon
"earth. And he shall become like a god in the under-

The scribe Ani passing through the door of the tomb; outside are his shadow and his
soul in the form of a human-headed bird. (From the *Papyrus of Ani*, plate 18.)

"world, and he shall never be turned back at any of
"the gates thereof." The words of the chapter have
great protective power (*i.e.*, are a charm of the greatest
importance) we are told, "for it was made by the cow
"for her son Rā when he was setting, and when his
"habitation was surrounded by a company of beings of
"fire." Now the cow is, of course, Isis-Hathor, and

both the words and the picture refer to some event in
the life of Rā, or Horus. It is quite evident that the
words of power, or charm, uttered by Isis-Hathor
delivered the god out of some trouble, and the idea is
that as it delivered the god, and was of benefit to him,
even so will it deliver the deceased and be of benefit to
him. The words of power read :—" O Amen, O Amen,
" who art in heaven, turn thy face upon the dead body
"of thy son, and make him sound and strong in the
"underworld." And again we are warned that the
words are "a great mystery " and that "the eye of no
"man whatsoever must see it, for it is a thing of
"abomination for [every man] to know it. Hide it,
" therefore ; the Book of the lady of the hidden temple
"is its name."

An examination of mummies of the late period
shews that the Egyptians did actually draw a figure of
the cow upon papyrus and lay it under the head of the
deceased, and that the cow is only one figure among
a number of others which were drawn on the same
papyrus. With the figures magical texts were inscribed
and in course of time, when the papyrus had been
mounted upon linen, it superseded the gold figure
of the cow which was fastened to the neck of the
deceased, and became, strictly speaking, an amulet,
though its usual name among archæologists is "hypocephalus." The figure on the opposite page well
illustrates the object. It will be noticed that the

Hypocephalus or object placed under the head of the deceased Shai-enen to keep warmth in the body.

hypocephalus is round; this is due to the fact that it
represents the pupil of the Eye of Horus, which from
time immemorial in Egypt was regarded as the source
of all generative power, and of reproduction and life.
The first group of gods are:—Nehebka offering to
Horus his Eye, a goddess with the Eye of Horus for
a head, the cow of Isis-Hathor described above, the
four children of Horus, two lions, a member of the
human body, the pylon of heads of Khnemu the god
of reproduction, and Horus-Rā. In the second are the
boat of the Sun being poled along by Horus, and the
boat of the Moon, with Harpocrates in the bow. In
the other scenes we have the god Khepera in his boat,
Horus in his boat, and Horus-Sept in his boat. The
god with two faces represents the double aspect of the
sun in setting and rising, and the god with the rams'
heads, who is being adored by apes, is a mystical form
of Khnemu, one of the great gods of reproduction,
who in still later times became the being whose name
under the form of Khnumis or Khnoubis occupied
such an important position among the magical names
which were in use among the Gnostics. The two
following prayers from the hypocephalus will illustrate
the words of power addressed to Amen, *i.e.*, the Hidden
One, quoted above :—1. " I am the Hidden One in the
" hidden place. I am a perfect spirit among the com-
" panions of Rā, and I have gone in and come forth
" among the perfect souls. I am the mighty Soul of

"saffron-coloured form. I have come forth from the
"underworld at pleasure. I have come. I have come
"forth from the Eye of Horus. I have come forth from
"the underworld with Rā from the House of the Great
"Aged One in Heliopolis. I am one of the spirits who
"come forth from the underworld: grant thou unto
"me the things which my body needeth, and heaven
"for my soul, and a hidden place for my mummy."
2. "May the god, who himself is hidden, and whose
"face is concealed, who shineth upon the world in his
"forms of existence, and in the underworld, grant that
"my soul may live for ever! May the great god in his
"disk give his rays in the underworld of Heliopolis!
"Grant thou unto me an entrance and an exit in the
"underworld without let or hindrance."

Chapter CLXIII. of the Book of the Dead was
written to prevent the body of a man mouldering
away in the underworld, and to deliver him from the
souls which were so unfortunate as to be shut in the
various places thereof, but in order to make it
thoroughly efficacious it was ordered to be recited over
three pictures: (1) a serpent with legs, having a disk
and two horns upon its head; (2) an *utchat*,[1] or Eye
of Horus, " in the pupil of which shall be a figure of
" the God of the lifted hand with the face of a divine
" soul, and having plumes and a back like a hawk ";
(3) an *utchat*, or Eye of Horus, "in the pupil of which

---

[1] See above, p. 55

"there shall be a figure of the God of the lifted hand
" with the face of the goddess Neith, and having plumes
" and a back like a hawk." If these things be done
for the deceased " he shall not be turned back at any
" gate of the underworld, he shall eat, and drink, and
" perform the natural functions of his body as he did
" when he was upon earth ; and none shall rise up to
" cry out against him ; and he shall be protected from
" the hands of the enemy for ever and ever." [1]

The words of power which form the CLXIVth
Chapter to be effectual had to be recited over a figure
of the goddess Mut which was to have three heads.
The first head was like that of the goddess Pekhat and
had plumes; the second was like that of a man and
had upon it the crowns of the South and North; the
third was like that of a vulture and had upon it
plumes; the figure had a pair of wings, and the claws
of a lion. This figure was painted in black, green, and
yellow colours upon a piece of *anes* linen ; in front of
it and behind it was painted a dwarf who wore plumes
upon his head. One hand and arm of each dwarf were
raised, and each had two faces, one being that of a
hawk and the other that of a man ; the body of each
was fat. These figures having been made, we are told
that the deceased shall be " like unto a god with the
"gods of the underworld; he shall never, never be
"turned back ; his flesh and his bones shall be like

[1] See *Chapters of Coming Forth by Day*, p. 292.

" those of one who hath never been dead ; he shall drink
" water at the source of the stream ; a homestead shall
" be given unto him in Sekhet-Aaru ; he shall become
" a star of heaven ; he shall set out to do battle with
" the serpent fiend Nekau and with Tar, who are in the
" underworld ; he shall not be shut in along with the
" souls which are fettered; he shall have power to
" deliver himself wherever he may be; and worms
" shall not devour him." [1]

Again, the words of power which form the CLXVth
Chapter to be effectual were ordered by the rubric to
" be recited over a figure of the God of the lifted hand,
" which shall have plumes upon its head ; the legs
" thereof shall be wide apart, and the middle portion of
" it shall be in the form of a beetle, and it shall be
" painted blue with a paint made of lapis-lazuli mixed
" with *qamai* water. And it shall be recited over a
" figure with a head like unto that of a man, and the
" hands and the arms thereof shall be stretched away from
" his body ; above its right shoulder shall there be the
" head of a ram, and above its left shoulder shall there
" be the head of a ram. And thou shalt paint the
" figure of the God of the lifted hand upon a piece of
" linen immediately over the heart of the deceased, and
" thou shalt paint the other over his breast; but let
" not the god Sukati who is in the underworld know
" it." If these things be done, " the deceased shall

---

[1] See *Chapters of Coming Forth by Day*, p. 294.

" drink water from the source of the stream, and he
" shall shine like the stars in the heavens above." It
is probable that Chapters CLXII.–CLXV. were composed at a comparatively late date.

Yet another example of the magical pictures of the
Book of the Dead must here be given. The vignette
of Chapter CXLVIII. contains pictures of seven cows
" and their bull," and of four rudders; the seven cows
have reference to the seven Hathor goddesses, the bull
is, of course, a form of Rā, and the four rudders refer to
the four quarters of the earth and to the four cardinal
points. The text of the Chapter contains the names of
the cows and of the bull, and of the rudders, and
certain prayers for sepulchral offerings. Now the
deceased would be provided with "abundance of food
" regularly and continually for ever," if the following
things were done for him. Figures of the cows and of
their bull and of the rudders were to be painted in
colours upon a board (?), and when Rā, the Sun-god,
rose upon them the friends of the deceased were to
place offerings before them; these offerings would be
received mystically by the gods and goddesses whom
the figures represented, and in return they would
bestow upon the deceased all the offerings or gifts of
meat and drink which he would require. Moreover,
" if this be done," we are told, " Rā shall be a rudder for
" the deceased, and he shall be a strength protecting
" him, and he shall make an end of all his enemies for

"him in the underworld, and in heaven, and upon
"earth, and in every place wherever he may enter."

We have seen above, in the description of the amulets
which the Egyptians used, how both the substance of
the amulet and the words which were inscribed upon it
possessed magical powers, but we may learn from several
instances given in the papyri that the written words
alone were sufficient in some cases to produce remarkable effects.   This is, of course, a very natural development, and charms or words of power which needed
nothing but to be written on papyrus or linen to produce a magical effect would be popular with all classes
of men and women, and especially among the poor and
the ignorant.   The written word has been regarded in
the East with reverence from time immemorial, and a
copy of a sacred writing or text is worn or carried
about to this day with much the same ideas and beliefs
about its power to protect as in the earliest times.   In
ancient Egypt the whole Book of the Dead, as well as
the various sections of it which are usually copied on
papyri, consisted of a series of " words of power," and
the modern Egyptian looks upon the Koran in the
same light as his ancestor looked upon the older work.
A curious passage in the text inscribed on the inside of
the pyramid of Unas reads (l. 583), " The bone and
" flesh which possess no writing are wretched, but,
" behold, the writing of Unas is under the great seal,
" and behold, it is not under the little seal."   It is

difficult to explain the passage fully, but there is no doubt that we have here an allusion to the custom of placing writings believed to be possessed of magical powers with the dead. Certain passages or sections of the religious books of ancient nations have always been held to be of more importance than others, and considering the great length of such compositions this is not to be wondered at. Among the Egyptians two forms of the LXIVth Chapter of the Book of the Dead were in use, and there is no doubt whatever that the shorter form, as far back as the Ist dynasty, about B.C. 4300, was intended to be a summary of the whole work, and that the recital of it was held to be as efficacious as the recital of all the rest of it.[1] It is a remarkable fact that this form is called "The Chapter of "knowing the 'Chapters of Coming Forth by Day' in "a single Chapter," and that it is declared to date from the time of Hesepti, a king of the Ist dynasty, about B.C. 4300, whilst the "finding" of the longer form is attributed to the reign of Men-kau-Rā (Mycerinus), a king of the IVth dynasty, about B.C. 3600. It is interesting to note how persistently certain chapters and formulæ occur in funeral papyri of different periods, and the explanation seems to be that a popular selection was made at an early date, and that this selection was

---

[1] In a similar way the Arabs attach as much importance to the *Fatha*, or opening chapter, and to the chapter which declares the Unity of God (CXII.), as to the rest of the *Koran*.

K

copied with such additions or omissions as the means of
the friends of the deceased allowed or made necessary.
One thing is quite certain : every man in Egypt died in
the firm belief that in the course of his journey into the
next world he would be provided with words of power
which would enable him to make his way thither un-
hindered, and give him abundance of meat and drink. We
may see this view which was held concerning words
of power from the following passages :—" May Thoth,
" who is filled and furnished with words of power,
" come and loose the bandages, even the bandages of
" Set which fetter my mouth. . . . Now as concerning
" the words of power and all the words which may be
" spoken against me, may the gods resist them, and
" may each and every one of the company of the gods
" withstand them." [1]   " Behold, I gather together the
" word of power from wherever it is, and from any
" person with whom it is, swifter than greyhounds and
" quicker than light." [2]   To the crocodile which cometh
to carry off from the deceased his words of power he
says, " Get thee back, return, get thee back, thou
" crocodile fiend Sui! Thou shalt not advance to me,
" for I live by reason of the words of power which I
" have with me. . . . Heaven hath power over its
" seasons, and the words of power have dominion over
" that which they possess; my mouth therefore shall
" have power over the words of power which are

[1] See *Chapters of Coming Forth by Day*, p. 70.   [2] *Ibid.*, p. 71

"therein."[1]   " I am clothed (?) and am wholly pro-
" vided with thy magical words, O Rā, the which are
" in the heaven above me, and in the earth beneath
" me."[2] To the two Sister-Mert goddesses the deceased
says, " My message to you is my words of power. I
" shine from the Sektet boat, I am Horus the son of
" Isis, and I have come to see my father Osiris."[3]   " I
" have become a spirit in my forms, I have gained the
" mastery over my words of power, and it is decreed
" for me to be a spirit."[4]   " Hail, thou that cuttest off
" heads, and slittest brows, thou who puttest away the
" memory of evil things from the mouth of the spirits
" by means of the words of power which they have
" within them, . . . let not my mouth be shut fast by
" reason of the words of power which thou hast within
" thee. . . . Get thee back, and depart before the words
" which the goddess Isis uttered when thou didst come
" to cast the recollection of evil things into the mouth
" of Osiris."[5]   On the amulet of the Buckle we have
inscribed the words, " May the blood of Isis, and the
" powers (?) of Isis, and the words of power of Isis be
" mighty to protect this mighty one," etc., and in the
address which Thoth makes to Osiris he says, " I am
" Thoth, the favoured one of Rā, the lord of might, who
" bringeth to a prosperous end that which he doeth, the
" mighty one of words of power, who is in the boat of

[1] See *Chapters of Coming Forth by Day*, p. 81.   [2] *Ibid.*, p. 81.
[3] *Ibid.*, p. 87.   [4] *Ibid.*, p. 129.   [5] *Ibid.*, p. 150.

" millions of years, the lord of laws, the subduer of
" the two lands," etc.[1]

From the above passages we not only learn how
great was the confidence which the deceased placed in
his words of power, but also that the sources from which
they sprang were the gods Thoth and Isis.   It will be
remembered that Thoth is called the " scribe of the
" gods," the " lord of writing," the " master of papyrus,"
the " maker of the palette and the ink-jar," the " lord
" of divine words," i.e., the holy writings or scriptures,
and as he was the lord of books and master of the
power of speech, he was considered to be the possessor
of all knowledge both human and divine.   At the
creation of the world it was he who reduced to words
the will of the unseen and unknown creative Power,
and who uttered them in such wise that the universe
came into being, and it was he who proved himself by
the exercise of his knowledge to be the protector and
friend of Osiris, and of Isis, and of their son Horus.
From the evidence of the texts we know that it was
not by physical might that Thoth helped these three
gods, but by giving them words of power and instruct-
ing them how to use them.   We know that Osiris
vanquished his foes, and that he reconstituted his body,
and became the king of the underworld and god of the
dead, but he was only able to do these things by means
of the words of power which Thoth had given to him,

---

[1] See *Chapters of Coming Forth by Day*, p. 340 f.

and which he had taught him to pronounce properly
and in a proper tone of voice. It is this belief which
makes the deceased cry out, " Hail, Thoth, who madest
" Osiris victorious over his enemies, make thou Ani to
" be victorious over his enemies in the presence of the
" great and sovereign princes who are in Tattu," or in any
other place. Without the words of power given to him
by Thoth, Osiris would have been powerless under the
attacks of his foes, and similarly the dead man, who
was always identified with Osiris, would have passed
out of existence at his death but for the words of power
provided by the writings that were buried with him.
In the Judgment Scene it is Thoth who reports to the
gods the result of the weighing of the heart in the
balance, and who has supplied its owner with the
words which he has uttered in his supplications, and
whatever can be said in favour of the deceased he says
to the gods, and whatever can be done for him he does.
But apart from being the protector and friend of Osiris,
Thoth was the refuge to which Isis fled in her trouble.
The words of a hymn declare that she knew " how to
" turn aside evil hap," and that she was " strong of
" tongue, and uttered the words of power which she
" knew with correct pronunciation, and halted not in her
" speech, and was perfect both in giving the command
" and in saying the word," [1] but this description only

[1] Chabas, *Revue Archéologique*, 1857, p. 65 ff.; Ledrain, *Monuments
Égyptiens*, pl. xxii. ff.; and for a recent translation see my *First
Steps in Egyptian*, pp. 179–188.

proves that she had been instructed by Thoth in the
art of uttering words of power with effect, and to him,
indeed, she owed more than this.   When she found the
dead body of her husband Osiris, she hovered about
over it in the form of a bird, making air by the beating
of her wings, and sending forth light from the sheen of
her feathers, and at length she roused the dead to life
by her words of power; as the result of the embrace
which followed this meeting Horus was born, and his
mother suckled him and tended him in her hiding-place
in the papyrus swamps.   After a time she was perse-
cuted by Set, her husband's murderer, who, it seems,
shut her and her son Horus up in a house as prisoners.
Owing, however, to the help which Thoth gave her, she
came forth by night and was accompanied on her
journey by seven scorpions,[1] called respectively Tefen,
Befen, Mestet, Mestetef, Petet, Thetet, and Matet, the
last three of which pointed out the way.   The guide of
the way brought her to the swamps of Per-sui,[2] and to
the town of the two goddesses of the sandals where the
swampy country of Athu begins.   Journeying on they
came to Teb,[3] where the chief of the district had a house
for his ladies; now the mistress of the house would not

[1] The story is told on the famous *Metternichstele*, ed. Golénischeff,
Leipzig, 1877.

[2] *I.e.*, Crocodilopolis.

[3] The city of the two sandals. The two sandals were made of
leather from the skin of the god Nehes or Set, the opponent of
Horus.

admit Isis on account of the scorpions that were with
her, for she had looked out of her door and watched
Isis coming. On this the scorpions took counsel together and wished to sting her by means of the scorpion
Tefen, but at this moment a poor woman who lived in
the marshes opened the door of her cottage to Isis,
and the goddess took shelter therein. Meanwhile the
scorpion had crept under the door into the house of
the governor, and stung the son of the lady of the
house, and also set the place on fire; no water could
quench the fire, and there was no rain to do it, for it
was not then the rainy season. Now these things
happened to the woman who had done no active harm
to Isis, and the poor creature wandered about the
streets of the city uttering loud cries of grief and
distress because she knew not whether her boy would
live or die.

When Isis saw this she was sorry for the child who
had been stung, and as he was blameless in the matter
of the door of his mother's house being shut in the face
of the goddess, she determined to save him. Thereupon
she cried out to the distraught mother, saying, " Come
" to me, come to me! For my word is a talisman
" which beareth life. I am a daughter well known in
" thy city also, and I will do away the evil by means
" of the word of my mouth which my father hath taught
" me, for I am the daughter of his own body." Then
Isis laid her hands upon the body of the boy, and

in order to bring back the spirit into his body
said—

"Come Tefen, appear upon the ground, depart hence,
" come not nigh !

"Come poison of Befen, appear upon the ground.   I
" am Isis, the goddess, the lady of words of power, who
" doeth deeds of magic, the words of whose voice are
" charms.

"Obey me, O every reptile that stingeth, and fall
" down headlong !

"O poison of [Mestet and] Mestetef, mount not
" upwards !

" O poison of Petet and Thetet, draw not nigh !

" O Matet, fall down headlong ! "

The goddess Isis then uttered certain words of the
charm which had been given to her by the god Seb
in order to keep poison away from her, and said, " Turn
away, get away, retreat, O poison," adding the words
" Mer-Rā " in the morning, and " The Egg of the Goose
" appeareth from out of the sycamore " in the evening,
as she turned to the scorpions.   Both these sentences
were talismans.   After this Isis lamented that she was
more lonely and wretched than all the people of Egypt,
and that she had become like an old man who hath
ceased to look upon and to visit fair women in their
houses ; and she ordered the scorpions to turn away
their looks from her and to show her the way to the
marshes and to the secret place which is in the city of

Khebt. Then the words of the cry, " The boy liveth,
" the poison dieth! As the sun liveth, so the poison
" dieth," were uttered, and the fire in the house of the
woman was extinguished, and heaven rejoiced at the
words of Isis. When Isis had said that the "son of
" the woman had been stung because his mother had
" shut the door of her house in her face, and had done
" nothing for her," the words of the cry, " The boy
" liveth and the poison dieth," were again uttered, and
the son of the woman recovered.

Isis then continues her narrative thus :—" I Isis
" conceived a child, and was great with child of Horus.
" I, a goddess, gave birth to Horus, the son of Isis,
" upon an island (or nest) in Athu the region of
" swamps ; and I rejoiced greatly because of this, for
" I regarded Horus as a gift which would repay me for
" the loss of his father. I hid him most carefully and
" concealed him in my anxiety, and indeed he was well
" hidden, and then I went away to the city of Am.
" When I had saluted the inhabitants thereof I turned
" back to seek the child, so that I might give him suck
" and take him in my arms again. But I found my
" sucking-child Horus, the fair golden one, well nigh
" dead! He had bedewed the ground with the water
" from his eye and with the foam from his lips, his
" body was stiff, his heart was still, and no muscle in
" any of his limbs moved.[1] Then I uttered a bitter cry

[1] This is an exact description of the state of an animal which has

" of grief, and the dwellers in the papyrus swamps ran
" to me straightway from out of their houses, and they
" bewailed the greatness of my calamity; but none of
" them opened his mouth to speak, for every one was in
" deep sorrow for me, and no man knew how to bring
" back life into Horus. Then there came to me a
" certain woman who was well known in her city, for
" she belonged to a noble family, and she tried to
" rekindle the life in Horus, but although her heart
" was full of her knowledge my son remained motion-
" less." Meanwhile the folk remarked that the son
of the divine mother Isis had been protected against
his brother Set, that the plants among which he had
been hidden could not be penetrated by any hostile
being, that the words of power of Temu, the father of
the gods, " who is in heaven," should have preserved
the life of Horus, that Set his brother could not possibly
have had access to where the child was, who, in any
case, had been protected against his wickedness; and
at length it was discovered that Horus had been stung
by a scorpion, and that the reptile " which destroyeth

been stung by the small black scorpion in Egypt and the Sûdân. I
saw Colonel W. H. Drage's dog "Shûbra" bitten at Merâwî in
September, 1897, by a black scorpion, and in about an hour she was
in the state of Horus as described above, and the whole camp was
distressed, for both master and dog were great favourites. When it
was no longer possible to administer spirit to her, Major G. R. Griffith
and others immersed her body in pails of very hot water for several
hours, and at sundown she was breathing comfortably, and she soon
afterwards recovered.

"the heart" had wounded him, and had probably killed him.

At this juncture Nephthys arrived, and went round about among the papyrus swamps weeping bitterly because of the affliction of her sister Isis; with her also was Serqet, the goddess of scorpions, who asked continually, "What hath happened to the child Horus?" Then Nephthys said to Isis, "Cry out in prayer unto "heaven, and let the mariners in the boat of Rā cease "to row, and let not the boat of Rā move further on "its course for the sake of the child Horus"; and forthwith Isis sent forth her cry up to heaven, and made her request come unto the "Boat of millions of years," and the Sun stood still and his boat moved not from its place by reason of the goddess's petition. Out from the boat came the god Thoth provided with magical powers, and bearing with him the great power to command in such wise that the words of his mouth must be fulfilled straightway; and he spake to Isis, saying, "O thou goddess Isis, whose mouth knoweth "how to utter charms (or talismans), no suffering shall "come upon thy child Horus, for his health and safety "depend upon the boat of Rā. I have come this day "in the divine boat of the Disk (Aten) to the place "where it was yesterday. When darkness (or night) "ruleth, the light shall vanquish it for the health (or "safety) of Horus for the sake of his mother Isis— "and similarly shall it happen unto every one who

" possesseth what is [here] written (?)." What took place next is, of course, evident. The child Horus was restored to life, to the great joy of his mother Isis, who was more indebted than ever to the god Thoth for coming to deliver her out of her trouble on the death of her son, just as he had done on the death of her husband. Now because Isis had revivified both her husband and her son by the words of power and talismans which she possessed, mortal man thought it was absolutely necessary for him to secure her favour and protection at any cost, for eternal life and death were in her hands. As time went on the Egyptians revered her more and more, and as she was the lady of the gods and of heaven, power equal to that possessed by Rā himself was ascribed to her. Indeed, according to a legend which has come down to us, and which written upon papyrus or linen formed a magical formula against the poison of reptiles of all kinds, she made a bold attempt to wrest the power of Rā from him and to make herself mistress of the universe. The way in which she did this is told in a hieratic papyrus preserved at Turin,[1] from which the following rendering has been made; the merit of first discovering the correct meaning of the text belongs to M. Lefébure.

[1] See Pleyte and Rossi, *Le Papyrus de Turin*, 1869–1876, pll. 31–37, and 131–138; see also Lefébure in *Ægyptische Zeitschrift*, 1883, p. 27 ff.; Wiedemann, *Religion der alten Ægypter*, 1890, p. 29 ff.; and my *Papyrus of Ani*, 1895, p. lxxxix., and *First Steps in Egyptian*, 1895, pp· 241–256.

THE LEGEND OF RĀ AND ISIS.

"The Chapter of the divine god, the self-created
"being, who made the heavens and the earth, and the
"winds [which give] life, and the fire, and the gods,
"and men, and beasts, and cattle, and reptiles, and the
"fowl of the air and the fish of the sea; he is the king
"of men and of gods, he hath one period of life (?) and
"with him periods of one hundred and twenty years
"each are but as years; his names are manifold and
"unknown, the gods even know them not.

"Now Isis was a woman who possessed words of
"power; her heart was wearied with the millions of
"men, therefore she chose the millions of the gods, but
"she esteemed more highly the millions of the spirits
"(khu). And she meditated in her heart, saying, 'Can-
"not I by means of the sacred name of God make
"myself mistress of the earth and become a goddess
"like unto Rā in heaven and upon earth?' Now
"behold, each day Rā entered at the head of his holy
"mariners and established himself upon the throne of
"the two horizons. Now the divine one (i.e., Rā) had
"grown old, he dribbled at the mouth, his spittle fell
"upon the earth, and his slobbering dropped upon the
"ground. And Isis kneaded it with earth in her
"hand, and formed thereof a sacred serpent in the
"form of a dart; she did not set it upright before her
"face, but let it lie upon the ground in the path

" whereby the great god went forth, according to his
" heart's desire, into his double kingdom. Now the
" holy god arose, and the gods who followed him as
" though he were Pharaoh went with him; and he came
" forth according to his daily wont; and the sacred
" serpent bit him: The flame of life departed from
" him, and he who dwelt among the cedars (?) was
" overcome. The holy god opened his mouth, and the
" cry of his majesty reached unto heaven; his company
" of gods said, 'What hath happened?' and his gods
" exclaimed, 'What is it?' But Rā could not answer,
" for his jaws trembled and all his members quaked;
" the poison spread swiftly through his flesh just as the
" Nile rusheth through all his land. When the great
" god had stablished his heart, he cried unto those who
" were in his train, saying, 'Come unto me, O ye who
" have come into being from my body, ye gods who
" have come forth from me, make ye known unto
" Khepera that a dire calamity hath fallen upon me.
" My heart perceiveth it, but my eyes see it not; my
" hand hath not caused it, nor do I know who hath
" done this unto me. Never have I felt such pain,
" neither can sickness cause more woe than this. I
" am a prince, the son of a prince, the sacred essence
" which hath proceeded from God. I am the great
" one, the son of the great one, and my father planned
" my name; I have multitudes of names and multitudes
" of forms, and my being is in every god. I have been

" proclaimed by the heralds Temu and Horus, and my
"father and my mother uttered my name; but it hath
"been hidden within me by him that begat me,
" who would not that the words of power of any seer
" should have dominion over me. I came forth to look
" upon that which I had made, I was passing through
" the world which I had created, when lo! something
"stung me, but what I know not. Is it fire? Is it
" water? My heart is on fire, my flesh quaketh, and
"trembling hath seized all my limbs. Let there be
" brought unto me my children, the gods, who possess
"the words of power and magical speech, and mouths
" which know how to utter them, and also powers
" which reach even unto the heavens.' Then the
" children of every god came unto him uttering cries
" of grief. And Isis also came, bringing with her her
" words of magical power, and her mouth was full of
" the breath of life; for her talismans vanquish the
" pains of sickness, and her words make to live again
" the throats of those who are dead. And she spake,
" saying, 'What hath come to pass, O holy Father?
" What hath happened? Is it that a serpent hath
" bitten thee, and that a thing which thou hast created
" hath lifted up his head against thee? Verily it shall
" be cast down by my effective words of power, and I
" will drive it away from before the sight of thy sun-
" beams.' The holy god opened his mouth and said,
" 'I was passing along my path, and I was going

"through the two regions of my lands according to "my heart's desire, to see that which I had created, "when lo! I was bitten by a serpent which I saw not. "Is it fire? Is it water? I am colder than water, I "am hotter than fire. All my flesh sweateth, I quake, "my eye hath no strength, I cannot see the sky, and "the sweat rusheth to my face even as in the time of "summer.' Then said Isis unto Rā, 'O tell me thy "name, holy Father, for whosoever shall be delivered "by thy name shall live.' And Rā said, 'I have made "the heavens and the earth, I have knit together the "mountains, I have created all that is above them, "I have made the water, I have made to come into "being the goddess Meht-urt, and I have made the "" Bull of his mother," from whom spring the delights "of love. I have made the heavens, I have stretched "out the two horizons like a curtain, and I have placed "the soul of the gods within them. I am he who, if "he openeth his eyes, doth make the light, and, if he "closeth them, darkness cometh into being. At his "command the Nile riseth, and the gods know not "his name. I have made the hours, I have created "the days, I bring forward the festivals of the year, "I create the Nile-flood. I make the fire of life, and "I provide food in the houses. I am Khepera in the "morning, I am Rā at noon, and I am Temu at even.' "Meanwhile the poison was not taken away from his "body, but it pierced deeper, and the great god could "no longer walk.

"Then said Isis unto Rā, 'What thou hast said is
"not thy name. O tell it unto me, and the poison
"shall depart; for he shall live whose name shall be
"revealed.' Now the poison burned like fire, and it
"was fiercer than the flame and the furnace, and the
"majesty of the great god said, 'I consent that Isis
"shall search into me, and that my name shall pass
"from me into her.' Then the god hid himself from
"the gods, and his place in the Boat of Millions of
"Years was empty. And when the time had arrived
"for the heart of Rā to come forth, Isis spake unto
"her son Horus, saying, 'The god hath bound himself
"by oath to deliver up his two eyes (i.e., the sun and
"moon).' Thus was the name of the great god taken
"from him, and Isis, the lady of words of magical
"power, said, 'Depart, poison, go forth from Rā. O
"Eye of Horus, go forth from the god, and shine outside
"his mouth. It is I who work, it is I who make to fall
"down upon the earth the vanquished poison, for the
"name of the great god hath been taken away from
"him. Let Rā live, and let the poison die! Let the
"poison die, and let Rā live!' These are the words
"of Isis, the mighty lady, the mistress of the gods, who
"knew Rā by his own name."

Now from a few words of text which follow the above
narrative we learn that the object of writing it was
not so much to instruct the reader as to make a magic
formula, for we are told that it was to be recited over

figures of Temu and Horus, and Isis and Horus, that
is to say, over figures of Temu the evening sun, Horus
the Elder, Horus the son of Isis, and Isis herself.
Temu apparently takes the place of Rā, for he represents
the sun as an old man, *i.e.*, Rā at the close of his daily
life when he has lost his strength and power. The
text is a charm or magical formula against snake bites,
and it was thought that the written letters, which
represented the words of Isis, would save the life of
any one who was snake-bitten, just as they saved the
life of Rā. If the full directions as to the use of the
figures of Temu, Isis, and the two Horus gods, were
known unto us we should probably find that they were
to be made to act in dumb show the scenes which
took place between Rā and Isis when the goddess
succeeded in taking from him his name. Thus we
have ample evidence that Isis possessed marvellous
magical powers, and this being so, the issues of life
and death, as far as the deceased was concerned, we
know from the texts to have been in her hands. Her
words of power, too, were a priceless possession, for
she obtained them from Thoth, who was the personifica-
tion of the mind and intelligence of the Creator, and
thus their origin was divine, and from this point of
view were inspired.

From a papyrus of the Ptolemaïc period we obtain
some interesting facts about the great skill in working
magic and about the knowledge of magical formulæ

which were possessed by a prince called Setnau Khā-
em-Uast. He knew how to use the powers of amulets
and talismans, and how to compose magical formulæ,
and he was master both of religious literature and of
that of the " double house of life," or library of magical
books. One day as he was talking of such things one
of the king's wise men laughed at his remarks, and
in answer Setnau said, " If thou wouldst read a book
" possessed of magical powers come with me and I will
" show it to thee, the book was written by Thoth him-
" self, and in it there are two formulæ. The recital of
" the first will enchant (or bewitch) heaven, earth, hell,
" sea, and mountains, and by it thou shalt see all the
" birds, reptiles, and fish, for its power will bring the
" fish to the top of the water. The recital of the second
" will enable a man if he be in the tomb to take the
" form which he had upon earth," etc. When questioned
as to where the book was, Setnau said that it was in
the tomb of Ptah-nefer-ka at Memphis. A little later
Setnau went there with his brother and passed three
days and three nights in seeking for the tomb of Ptah-
nefer-ka, and on the third day they found it; Setnau
recited some words over it, and the earth opened and
they went down to the place where the book was.
When the two brothers came into the tomb they found
it to be brilliantly lit up by the light which came forth
from the book; and when they looked they saw not only
Ptah-nefer-ka, but his wife Ahura, and Merhu their

son. Now Ahura and Merhu were buried at Coptos
but their doubles had come to live with Ptah-nefer-ka
by means of the magical power of Thoth. Setnau told
them that he had come to take away the book, but
Ahura begged him not to do so, and related to him the
misfortunes which had already followed the possession
of it. She was, it seems, the sister of Ptah-nefer-ka
whom she married, and after the birth of her son
Merhu, her husband seemed to devote himself ex-
clusively to the study of magical books, and one day
a priest of Ptah promised to tell him where the magical
book described above might be found if he would give
him a hundred pieces of silver, and provide him with two
handsome coffins. When the money and the coffins had
been given to him, the priest of Ptah told Ptah-nefer-ka
that the book was in an iron box in the middle of the
river at Coptos. "The iron box is in a bronze box, the
"bronze box is in a box of palm-tree wood, the palm-
"tree wood box is in a box of ebony and ivory, the
"ebony and ivory box is in a silver box, the silver box
"is in a gold box, and in the gold (sic) box lies the book.
"The box wherein is the book is surrounded by swarms
"of serpents and scorpions and reptiles of all kinds, and
"round it is coiled a serpent which cannot die." Ptah-
nefer-ka told his wife and the king what he had heard,
and at length set out for Coptos with Ahura and Merhu
in the royal barge; having arrived at Coptos he went
to the temple of Isis and Harpocrates and offered up

a sacrifice and poured out a libation to these gods.
Five days later the high priest of Coptos made for him
the model of a floating stage and figures of workmen
provided with tools; he then recited words of power
over them and they became living, breathing men, and
the search for the box began. Having worked for
three days and three nights they came to the place
where the box was. Ptah-nefer-ka dispersed the serpents and scorpions which were round about the nest
of boxes by his words of power, and twice succeeded
in killing the serpent coiled round the box, but it came
to life again; the third time he cut it into two pieces,
and laid sand between them, and this time it did not
take its old form again. He then opened the boxes
one after the other, and taking out the gold box with
the book inside it carried it to the royal barge. He
next read one of the two formulæ in it and so enchanted
or bewitched the heavens and the earth that he learned
all their secrets; he read the second and he saw the
sun rising in the heavens with his company of the gods,
etc. His wife Ahura then read the book and saw
all that her husband had seen. Ptah-nefer-ka then
copied the writings on a piece of new papyrus, and
having covered the papyrus with incense dissolved it
in water and drank it; thus he acquired the knowledge
which was in the magical book. Meanwhile these acts
had stirred the god Thoth to wrath, and he told Râ
what Ptah-nefer-ka had done. As a result the decree

went forth that Ptah-nefer-ka and his wife and child should never return to Memphis, and on the way back to Coptos Ahura and Merhu fell into the river and were drowned; and while returning to Memphis with the book Ptah-nefer-ka himself was drowned also. Setnau, however, refused to be diverted from his purpose, and he insisted on having the book which he saw in the possession of Ptah-nefer-ka; the latter then proposed to play a game of draughts and to let the winner have the book. The game was for fifty-two points, and although Ptah-nefer-ka tried to cheat Setnau, he lost the game. At this juncture Setnau sent his brother Anhaherurau up to the earth to bring him his talismans of Ptah and his other magical writings, and when he returned he laid them upon Setnau, who straightway flew up to heaven grasping the wonderful book in his hand. As he went up from the tomb light went before him, and the darkness closed in behind him; but Ptah-nefer-ka said to his wife, " I will make "him bring back this book soon, with a knife and a "rod in his hand and a vessel of fire upon his head." Of the bewitchment of Setnau by a beautiful woman called Tabubu and of his troubles in consequence thereof we need make no mention here: it is sufficient to say that the king ordered him to take the book back to its place, and that the prophecy of Ptah-nefer-ka was fulfilled.[1]

[1] For translations see Brugsch, *Le Roman de Setnau* (in *Revue*

In connexion with the subject of the magical powers of Isis must be briefly mentioned the curious small stelæ, with rounded tops, on the front of which are inscribed figures of the god Horus standing upon crocodiles : they are usually known as " cippi of Horus." The largest and finest example of this remarkable class of object is the famous " Metternichstele," which was found in the year 1828 during the building of a cistern in a Franciscan monastery in Alexandria, and was presented by Muhammad Ali Pasha to Prince Metternich. We are fortunately enabled to date the stele, for the name of Nectanebus I., the last but one of the native kings of Egypt, who reigned from B.C. 378 to B.C. 360, occurs on it, and we know from many sources that such a monument could have been produced only about this period. From the two illustrations of it here given we see that it is both sculptured and engraved with figures of many of the gods of ancient Egypt, gods well known from the monuments of the earlier dynasties, and also with figures of a series of demons and monsters and animals which have both mythological and magical importance. Many of these are accompanied by texts containing magical formulæ,

Archéologique, 2nd series, vol. xvi., 1867, p. 161 ff.); Maspero, *Contes Égyptiens*, Paris, 1882, pp. 45–82 ; *Records of the Past*, vol. iv., pp. 129–148; and for the original Demotic text see Mariette, *Les Papyrus du Musée de Boulaq*, tom. i., 1871, pll. 29–32 ; Revillout, *Le Roman de Setna*, Paris, 1877 ; Hess, *Roman von Sfne Ha-m-us*, Leipzig, 1888.

magical names, and mythological allusions. In the
principal scene we see Horus, or Harpocrates, standing
upon two crocodiles ; on his brow is the uraeus, and
he wears on the right side of his head the lock of
hair emblematic of youth. In his hands he grasps
serpents, a lion, and an antelope, and it is clear by the
look on his face that he is in no wise afraid of them.
Above his head is a bearded head, which is usually said
to represent that of Bes. On his right are :—(1) an
utchat,[1] with human hands and arms; (2) Horus-Rā,
hawk-headed, and wearing the sun's disk and uraeus,
and standing on a serpent coiled up; (3) Osiris, in the
form of a hawk standing upon a sceptre, and wearing
the *atef* crown; (4) The goddess Isis standing upon
a serpent coiled up; (5) The goddess Nekhebet, in the
form of a vulture, standing upon a papyrus sceptre.
On his left are :—(1) An *utchat* with human hands
and arms; (2) a papyrus standard with plumes and
menats[2]; (3) the god Thoth standing upon a serpent
coiled up; (4) the goddess Uatchet, in the form of a
serpent, standing upon a papyrus sceptre. Now Horus
typifies youth and strength and the rising sun, and
the head above him is probably intended to represent
that of Rā (or Bes) as an old man; the allusion here
is clearly to the god who " is old at eventide and who
"becomes young again." The *utchats* and the figures
of the gods symbolize the solar powers and the deities

[1] See above, p. 55.   [2] See above, p. 60.

Cippus of Horus. (See *Metternichstele*, ed. Golénischeff, plate 1.)

who are masters of the words of power, both in the
South and in the North, by which the young god
Horus vanquishes all hostile animals, reptiles, and
creeping things which live in water and on land.
Above and about this scene are several rows of figures
of gods and sketches of mythological scenes; many of
which are evidently taken from the vignettes of the
Book of the Dead, and the object of all of the latter
is to prove that light overcomes darkness, that good
vanquishes evil, and that renewed life comes after
death.   The texts which fill all the spaces not occupied
by figures describe certain incidents of the eternal
combat which Horus wages against his brother Set,
and tell the story of the wanderings of Isis with her
son Horus and of her sufferings in the country of the
papyrus swamps, a sketch of which we have given
above (see pp. 130–136); besides these, prayers to certain gods are introduced.   The whole monument is
nothing but a talisman, or a gigantic amulet engraved
with magical figures and words of power, and it was,
undoubtedly, placed in some conspicuous place in a
courtyard or in a house to protect the building and its
inmates from the attacks of hostile beings, visible and
invisible, and its power was believed to be invincible.
There is not a god of any importance whose figure is
not on it, and there is not a demon, or evil animal or
reptile, who is not depicted upon it in a vanquished
state ; the knowledge of the ancient Egyptian mythology

and the skill shewn by the designer of this talisman
are very remarkable. The small cippi of Horus contain
nothing but extracts from the scenes and texts which
we find on the "Metternichstele," and it, or similar
objects, undoubtedly formed the source from which so
many of the figures of the strange gods which are found
on Gnostic gems were derived. Certain of the figures
of the gods on the cippi were cast in bronze in the
Ptolemaïc and Roman periods, or hewn in stone, and
were buried in tombs and under the foundations of
houses to drive away any of the fiends who might come
to do harm either to the living or the dead.

The Arab historian Mas'ûdî has preserved[1] a curious
legend of the talismans which were employed by Alexander the Great to protect the city of Alexandria whilst
it was being built, and as the legend is of Egyptian
origin, and dates from a period not greatly removed
from that in which the Metternich stele was made, it
is worthy of mention. When the foundations of the
city had been laid, and the walls had begun to rise up,
certain savage animals came up each night from the
sea, and threw down everything which had been built
during the day; watchmen were appointed to drive
them away, but in spite of this each morning saw the
work done during the previous day destroyed. After
much thought Alexander devised a plan whereby he

[1] See *Les Prairies d'Or*, ed. B. de Meynard and Pavet de Courteille,
Paris, 1861, tom. ii. p. 425 ff.

Cippus of Horus. (See *Metternichstele*, ed. Golénischeff, plate 3.)

might thwart the sea monsters, and he proceeded to carry it into effect. He made a box ten cubits long and five cubits wide with sides made of sheets of glass fastened into frames by means of pitch, resin, etc. In this box Alexander placed himself, together with two skilful draughtsmen, and having been closed it was towed out to sea by two vessels; and when weights of iron, lead, and stone had been attached to the under part of it, it began to sink, being guided to the place which Alexander wished it to reach by means of cords which were worked from the ships. When the box touched the bottom of the sea, thanks to the clearness of the glass sides and the water of the sea, Alexander and his two companions were able to watch the various marine monsters which passed by, and he saw that although they had human bodies they had the heads of beasts; some had axes, some had saws, and some had hammers, and they all closely resembled workmen. As they passed in front of the box Alexander and his two draughtsmen copied their forms upon paper with great exactness, and depicted their hideous countenances, and stature, and shape; this done, a signal was made, and the box was drawn up to the surface. As soon as Alexander reached the land he ordered his stone and metal workers to make reproductions of the sea monsters according to the drawings which he and his friends had made, and when they were finished he caused them to be set up on pedestals along the sea-shore, and continued his work of building the city. When the night came, the sea monsters appeared as usual, but as soon as they saw that figures of themselves had been put up on the shore they returned at once to the water and did not shew themselves again. When, however, the city had been built and was inhabited, the sea monsters made their appearance again, and each morning a considerable number of people were found to be missing; to prevent this Alexander placed talismans upon the pillars which, according to Mas'ûdî, were there in his day. Each pillar was in the shape of an arrow, and was eighty cubits in height, and rested upon a plinth of brass; the talismans were placed at their bases, and were in the form of figures or statues of certain beings with suitable inscriptions, and as they were put in position after careful astronomical calculations had been made for the purpose we may assume that they produced the effect desired by the king.

CHAPTER V.

MAGICAL NAMES.

THE Egyptians, like most Oriental nations, attached very great importance to the knowledge of names, and the knowledge of how to use and to make mention of names which possessed magical powers was a necessity both for the living and the dead. It was believed that if a man knew the name of a god or a devil, and addressed him by it, he was bound to answer him and to do whatever he wished; and the possession of the knowledge of the name of a man enabled his neighbour to do him good or evil. The name that was the object of a curse brought down evil upon its owner, and similarly the name that was the object of a blessing or prayer for benefits secured for its master many good things. To the Egyptian the name was as much a part of a man's being as his soul, or his double (KA), or his body, and it is quite certain that this view was held by him in the earliest times. Thus in the text which is inscribed on the walls inside [1] the pyramid

[1] Line 169.

M

of Pepi I., king of Egypt about B.C. 3200, we read,
"Pepi hath been purified. He hath taken in his
"hand the *māh* staff, he hath provided himself with
"his throne, and he hath taken his seat in the
"boat of the great and little companies of the gods.
"Rā maketh Pepi to sail to the West, he stablisheth
"his seat above those of the lords of doubles, and
"he writeth down Pepi at the head of those who live.
"The doors of Pekh-ka which are in the abyss open
"themselves to Pepi, the doors of the iron which
"is the ceiling of the sky open themselves to
"Pepi, and he passeth through them; he hath his
"panther skin upon him, and the staff and whip are
"in his hand. Pepi goeth forward with his flesh, Pepi
"is happy with his name, and he liveth with his *ka*
"(double)." Curiously enough only the body and
name and double of the king are mentioned, just as
if these three constituted his whole economy; and it
is noteworthy what importance is attached to the name
in this passage. In the text from the pyramid of
another king[1] we have a prayer concerning the preservation of the name, which is of such interest that
a rendering of it in full is here given: it reads, "O
"Great Company of the gods who dwell in Annu
"(Heliopolis), grant that Pepi Nefer-ka-Rā may flourish
"(*literally* 'germinate'), and that his pyramid, his ever-
"lasting building, may flourish, even as the name of

[1] Pepi II. (ed. Maspero, l. 669, ff. Recueil, tom. xii. 1892, p. 146).

" Temu, the chief of the nine gods, doth flourish. If
" the name of Shu, the lord of the upper shrine in
" Annu, flourisheth, then Pepi shall flourish, and his
" pyramid, his everlasting building, shall flourish! If
" the name of Tefnut, the lady of the lower shrine in
" Annu, flourisheth, the name of Pepi shall be estab-
" lished, and this his pyramid shall be established
" to all eternity! If the name of Seb flourisheth
" at the 'homage of the earth,' then the name of Pepi
" shall flourish, and this his pyramid shall flourish, and
" this his building shall flourish unto all eternity! If
" the name of Nut in the House of Shenth in Annu
" flourisheth, the name of Pepi shall flourish, and this
" his pyramid shall flourish, and this his building shall
" flourish unto all eternity! If the name of Osiris
" flourisheth in the nome of Abydos, then the name of
" Pepi shall flourish, and this his pyramid shall flourish,
" and this his building shall flourish unto all eternity!
" If the name of Osiris Khent-Amentet flourisheth,
" then the name of Pepi shall flourish, and this his
" pyramid shall flourish, and this his building shall
" flourish unto all eternity! If the name of Set, the
" dweller in Nubt (Ombos) flourisheth, then the name
" of Pepi shall flourish, and this his pyramid shall
" flourish, and this his building shall flourish unto all
" eternity! If the name of Horus flourisheth, then the
" name of Pepi shall flourish, and this his pyramid shall
" flourish, and this his building shall flourish unto all

" eternity! If the name of Rā flourisheth in the
" horizon, then the name of Pepi shall flourish, and
" this his pyramid shall flourish, and this his building
" shall flourish unto all eternity! If the name of
" Khent-merti flourisheth in Sekhem (Letopolis), then
" the name of Pepi shall flourish, and this his pyramid
" shall flourish, and this his building shall flourish
" unto all eternity! If the name of Uatchet in Tep
" flourisheth, then the name of Pepi shall flourish, and
" this his pyramid shall flourish, and this his building
" shall flourish unto all eternity!" The above prayer
or formula was the origin of most of the prayers and
texts which had for their object the "making the name
to germinate *or* flourish," and which were copied so
frequently in the Saïte, Ptolemaïc, and Roman periods.
All these compositions show that from the earliest to
the latest times the belief as to the importance of the
preservation of the name never changed in Egypt, and
the son who assisted in keeping green his father's
name, and in consequence his memory, performed a
most meritorious duty. But in the present chapter we
are not so much concerned with the ordinary as with
the extraordinary uses to which a name might be put,
and the above facts have only been mentioned to prove
that a man's name was regarded as an essential part
of himself, and that the blotting out of the name of
an individual was synonymous with his destruction.
Without a name no man could be identified in the

judgment, and as a man only came into being upon this earth when his name had been pronounced, so the future life could only be attained after the gods of the world beyond the grave had become acquainted with it and had uttered it.

According to the story of the Creation which is related in the Papyrus of Nesi-Amsu,[1] before the world and all that therein is came into being, only the great god Neb-er-tcher existed, for even the gods were not born. Now when the time had come for the god to create all things he says, " I brought (*i.e.*, fashioned) my " mouth, and I uttered my own name as a word of " power, and thus I evolved myself under the evolu- " tions of the god Khepera, and I developed myself out " of the primeval matter which had evolved multitudes " of evolutions from the beginning of time. Nothing " existed on this earth [before me], I made all things. " There was none other who worked with me at that " time." Elsewhere, that is to say, in the other version of the story, the god Khepera says, " I developed " myself from the primeval matter which I made, I " developed myself out of the primeval matter. My " name is ' Osiris,' the germ of primeval matter." Here, then, we have a proof that the Egyptians regarded the creation as the result of the utterance of the name of the god Neb-er-tcher or Khepera by himself. Again, in the story of Rā and Isis, given in the preceding

[1] See my paper in *Archæologia*, Vol. LII., London, 1891.

chapter, we have seen that although Isis was able to
make a serpent and to cause it to bite Rā, and to make
him very ill, she was powerless to do as she wished in
heaven and upon earth until she had persuaded the god
to reveal to her his name by which he ruled the
universe.   In yielding up his name to the goddess he
placed himself in her power, and in this example we
have a striking instance of the belief that the knowledge of the name of god, or devil, or human being,
implied dominion over that being.   We have seen elsewhere that Rā, the type and symbol of God, is described
as the god of "many names," and in that wonderful
composition the XVIIth Chapter of the Book of the
Dead,[1] we have the following statement:—" I am the
" great god Nu, who gave birth unto himself, and who
" made his name to become the company of the gods."
Then the question, " What does this mean ?" or " Who
" is this ?" is asked.   And this is the answer: " It is
" Rā, the creator of the name[s] of his limbs, which
" came into being in the form of the gods who are in
" the following of Rā."   From this we see that all the
" gods " of Egypt were merely personifications of the
NAMES of Rā, and that each god was one of his members, and that a name of a god was the god himself.
Without the knowledge of the names of the gods and
devils of the underworld the dead Egyptian would have
fared badly, for his personal liberty would have been

[1] See *Chapters of Coming Forth by Day*, p. 49.

fettered, the roads and paths would have been blocked to him, the gates of the mansions of the underworld would have been irrevocably shut in his face, and the hostile powers which dogged his footsteps would have made an end of him; these facts are best illustrated by the following examples :—

When the deceased comes to the Hall of Judgment, at the very beginning of his speech he says, "Homage "to thee, O Great God, thou Lord of Maāti, I have "come to thee, O my Lord, and I have brought myself "hither that I may behold thy beauties. I know thee, "and I know thy name, and I know the names of the "two and forty gods who exist with thee in this Hall "of Maāti."[1] But although the gods may be favourable to him, and he be found righteous in the judgment, he cannot make his way among the other gods of the underworld without a knowledge of the names of certain parts of the Hall of Maāti. After the judgment he acquires the mystical name of " He who is equipped "with the flowers and the dweller in his olive tree," and it is only after he has uttered this name that the gods say "Pass onwards." Next the gods invite him to enter the Hall of Maāti, but he is not allowed to pass in until he has, in answer to questions asked by the bolts, lintels, threshold, fastenings, socket, door-leaves, and door-posts, told their names. The floor of the Hall will not permit him to walk upon it unless he

[1] See *Chapters of Coming Forth by Day*, p. 191.

tells not only its name, but also the mystical names of his two legs and feet wherewith he is about to tread upon it.   When all this has been done the guardian of the Hall says to him, "I will not announce thy name "[to the god] unless thou tellest me my name"; and the deceased replies, "'Discerner of hearts and searcher "of the reins' is thy name."   In reply to this the guardian says, "If I announce thy name thou must "utter the name of the god who dwelleth in his hour," and the deceased utters the name "Māau-Taui."   But still the guardian is not satisfied, and he says, "If I "announce thy name thou must tell me who is he "whose heaven is of fire, whose walls [are surmounted "by] living uraei, and the floor of whose house is a "stream of water.   Who is he, I say ? (*i.e.*, what is his "name ?)"   But the deceased has, of course, learnt the name of the Great God, and he replies, "Osiris."   The guardian of the Hall is now content, and he says, "Advance, verily thy name shall be mentioned to "him"; and he further promises that the cakes, and ale, and sepulchral meals which the deceased shall enjoy shall come from the "Eye of Rā."

In another Chapter[1] the deceased addresses seven gods, and says, "Hail, ye seven beings who make "decrees, who support the Balance on the night of the "judgment of the Utchat, who cut off heads, who hack "necks in pieces, who take possession of hearts by

---

[1] See *Chapters of Coming Forth by Day*, p. 128.

" violence and rend the places where hearts are fixed,
" who make slaughterings in the Lake of Fire, I know
" you, and I know your names; therefore know ye me,
" even as I know your names." The deceased, having
declared that the seven gods know his name and he
their names, has no further apprehension that evil will
befall him.

In one portion of the kingdom of Osiris there existed
seven halls or mansions through which the deceased
was anxious to pass, but each of the gates was guarded
by a doorkeeper, a watcher, and a herald, and it
required special provision on the part of the deceased
to satisfy these beings that he had a right to pass them.
In the first place, figures of the seven gates had to be
made in some substance (or painted upon papyrus), as
well as a figure of the deceased: the latter was made to
approach each of the gates and to stand before it and to
recite an address which had been specially prepared
for the purpose. Meanwhile the thigh, the head, the
heart, and the hoof of a red bull were offered at each
gate, as well as a very large number of miscellaneous
offerings which need not be described in detail. But
all these ceremonies would not help the deceased to
pass through the gates, unless he knew the names of
the seven doorkeepers, and the seven watchers, and the
seven heralds who guarded them. The gods of the first
gate were :—Sekhet-hra-āsht-aru, Semetu, and Hu-
khẹru ; those of the second, Tun-hāt, Seqet-hra, and

Sabes; of the third, Am-huat-ent-pehfi, Res-hra, and Uāau; of the fourth, Khesef-hra-āsht-kheru, Res-ab, and Neteka-hra-khesef-atu; of the fifth, Ānkh-em-fentu, Ashebu, and Tebherkehaat; of the sixth, Akentauk-ha-kheru, An-hra, and Metes-hra-ari-she; of the seventh, Metes-sen, Āāa-kheru, and Khesef-hra-khemiu. And the text, which the deceased recites to the Halls collectively, begins, "Hail, ye Halls! Hail, ye who "made the Halls for Osiris! Hail, ye who watch "your Halls! Hail, ye who herald the affairs of the "two lands for the god Osiris each day, the deceased "knoweth you, and he knoweth your names."[1] The names having been uttered, and the addresses duly recited, the deceased went wherever he pleased in the seven Halls of Osiris.

But beside the seven halls the deceased had to pass through the twenty-one hidden pylons of the house of Osiris in the Elysian Fields, and in order to do so he had to declare the names of the pylon and the door-keeper of each, and to make a short address besides. Thus to the first pylon he says, "I have made my way, "I know thee and I know thy name, and I know the "name of the god who guardeth thee. Thy name is "'Lady of tremblings, with lofty walls, the sovereign "lady, the mistress of destruction, who setteth in order "the words which drive back the whirlwind and the "storm, who delivereth from destruction him that

---

[1] See *Chapters of Coming Forth by Day*, p. 241.

"travelleth along the way'; and the name of thy door-
"keeper is Neri." At the second pylon he says, "I
"have made [my] way, I know thee, and I know thy
"name, and I know the name of the god who guardeth
"thee. Thy name is 'Lady of heaven, the mistress of
"the world, who devoureth with fire, the lady of
"mortals, who knoweth mankind.' The name of thy
"doorkeeper is Mes-Ptah," and so on at each of the
pylons. In the later and longer version of the chapter
which was written to supply the deceased with this
knowledge he informs the god of each pylon what
purification he has undergone; thus to the god of the
first pylon he says, "I have anointed myself with *hāti*
"unguent [made from] the cedar, I have arrayed myself
"in apparel of *menkh* (linen), and I have with me my
"sceptre made of *heti* wood." After the speech the
god of the pylon says, "Pass on, then, thou art pure."

When we remember that one of the oldest beliefs as
to the future life made it appear that it would be lived
by man in the Sekhet-Aaru, or Field of Reeds, a region
which, as we know from the drawings of it which have
come down to us, was intersected by canals and
streams, it is at once clear that in order to pass from
one part of it to another the deceased would need a
boat. Even assuming that he was fortunate enough to
have made his own way into this region, it was not
possible for him to take a boat with him. To meet
this difficulty a boat and all its various parts were

drawn upon the papyrus, upon which the selection of
Chapters from the Book of the Dead had been inscribed
for him, and a knowledge of the text of the chapter
which belonged to it made the drawing to become an
actual boat.   But before he could enter it, the post
to which it was tied up, and every part of the boat
itself, demanded that he should tell them their names,
thus :—

Post at which to tie up. " Tell me my name."
D.[1] " Lord of the two lands, dweller in the shrine,"
is thy name.

Rudder. " Tell me my name."   D. " Leg of Hāpiu " is
thy name.

Rope. " Tell me my name."   D. " Hairs with which
Anpu finisheth the work of my embalmment " is
thy name.

Oar-rests. " Tell us our name."   D. " Pillars of the
underworld " is your name.

Hold. " Tell me my name."   D. " Akau " is thy name.

Mast. " Tell me my name."   D. " Bringer back of the
lady after her departure " is thy name.

Lower deck. " Tell me my name."   D. " Standard of
Ap-uat " is thy name.

Upper Post. " Tell me my name."   D. " Throat of
Mestha " is thy name.

Sail. " Tell me my name."   D. " Nut " is thy name.

Leather Straps. " Tell us our name."   D. " Those who

---

[1] D. = the deceased.

are made from the hide of the Mnevis Bull, which was burned by Suti," is your name.

Paddles. "Tell us our name." D. "Fingers of Horus the firstborn " is your name.

Pump (?). "Tell me my name. D. "The hand of Isis, which wipeth away the blood of the Eye of Horus," is thy name.

Planks. "Tell us our names." D. "Mestha, Hāpi, Tuamutef, Qebhsennuf, Haqau, Thet-em-āua, Maa-an-tef, Ari-nef-tchesef," are your names.

Bows. "Tell us our name. D. "He who is at the head of his nomes " is your name.

Hull. "Tell me my name." D. "Mert " is thy name.

Rudder. "Tell me my name." D. "Āqa " is thy name; "Shiner in the water, hidden beam," is thy name.

Keel. "Tell me my name." D. "Thigh of Isis, which Rā cut off with the knife to bring blood into the Sektet boat," is thy name.

Sailor. "Tell me my name." D. "Traveller " is thy name.

Wind. "Tell me my name." D. "The North Wind, which cometh from Tem to the nostrils of Osiris," is thy name.

And when the deceased had declared to these their names, before he could set out on his journey he was obliged to tell the river, and the river-banks, and the ground their mystical names. This done, the boat admitted him as a passenger, and he was able to sail about to any part of the Elysian Fields at will.

But among the beings whom the deceased wished to avoid in the underworld were the beings who "lay "snares, and who work the nets, and who are fishers," and who would draw him into their nets. It seems as if it were absolutely necessary that he should fall in with these beings and their nets, for a whole chapter of the Book of the Dead was written with the view of enabling him to escape from them unharmed; the god their leader is called "the god whose face is "behind him," and "the god who hath gained the "mastery over his heart." To escape from the net which was worked by "the fishers who lay snares with "their nets and who go round about in the chambers "of the waters," the deceased had to know the names of the net, and of the ropes, and of the pole, and of the hooks, and of each and every part of it; without this knowledge nothing could save him from calamity. We unfortunately understand very few of the allusions to mythological events which are contained in the names of the various parts of the machinery which work the net, but it is quite certain that they have reference to certain events in the lives of the gods who are mentioned, and that these were well known to the writers and readers of religious texts.

From the above descriptions of the means whereby the deceased made his way through the gates and the

halls of the underworld and escaped from the fowler
and his net, it will be readily understood that the
knowledge of the name alone was, in some cases, sufficient to help him out of his difficulties ; but in others
it was necessary to have the name which was possessed of magical power inscribed upon some object,
amulet or otherwise. Moreover, some gods and devils
were thought to have the power to assume different
forms, and as each form carried with it its own name,
to have absolute power over a god of many forms it
was necessary to know all his names. Thus in the
" Book of Overthrowing Āpep "[1] we are told not only
to make a wax figure of the monster, but also to write
his name upon it, so that when the figure is destroyed
by being burnt in the fire his name also may be
destroyed; this is a striking example of the belief that
the name was an integral part of the economy of a
living creature. But Apep possessed many forms
and therefore many names, and unless he could be
invoked by these names he still had the power to do
evil; the above-mentioned book[2] therefore supplies us
with a list of his names, among which occur the following :—" Tutu (*i.e.*, Doubly evil one), Hau-hra (*i.e.*,
" Backward Face), Hemhemti (*i.e.*, Roarer), Qetu (*i.e.*,
" Evil-doer), Āmam (*i.e.*, Devourer), Saatet-ta (*i.e.*, Dark-
" ener of earth), Iubani, Khermuti, Unti, Karaüememti,

---

[1] *Papyrus of Nesi-Amsu*, col. xxiii. l. 6. (*Archæologia*, vol. LII.)
[2] *Ibid.*, col. xxxii. l. 13 f.

"Khesef-hra, Sekhem-hra, Khak-áb, Nāi, Uai, Beteshu,
"Kharebutu the fourfold fiend," etc. All these names
represent, as may be seen from the few of which translations are given, various aspects of Āpep, the devil
of thunder, lightning, cloud, rain, mist, storm, and the
like, and the anxiety to personify these so that the
personifications might be attacked by means of magical
ceremonies and words of power seems positively childish.

Passing now to certain chapters of the Book of the
Dead which are rich in names of magical power,[1] we
notice that the god Amen, whose name meant the
"hidden one," possessed numerous names, upon the
knowledge of which the deceased relied for protection.
Thus he says, "O Amen,[2] Amen; O Re-Iukasa; O
"God, Prince of the gods of the east, thy name is
"Na-ari-k, or (as others say) Ka-ari-ka, Kasaika is thy
"name. Arethikasathika is thy name. Amen-na-an-
"ka-entek-share, or (as others say) Thek-share-Amen-
"kerethi, is thy name. O Amen, let me make suppli-
"cation unto thee, for I, even I, know thy name.
"Amen is thy name. Ireqai is thy name. Marqathai
"is thy name. Rerei is thy name. Nasaqbubu is thy
"name. Thanasa-Thanasa is thy name. Shareshatha-
"katha is thy name. O Amen, O Amen, O God, O
"God, O Amen, I adore thy name." In another
place [3] the deceased addresses Sekhet-Bast-Rā, saying,

---

[1] Chapters CLXII., CLXIII., CLXIV., CLXV.
[2] See *Chapters of Coming Forth by Day*, p. 295.   [3] *Ibid.*, p. 293.

" Thou art the fire-goddess Ami-seshet, whose oppor-
" tunity escapeth her not ; thy name is Kaharesapusa-
" remkakaremet.   Thou art like unto the mighty flame
" of Saqenaqat which is in the bow of the boat of
" thy father Harepukakashareshabaiu, for behold, thus
" is [the name uttered] in the speech of the Negroes,
" and of the Anti, and of the people of Nubia. . . .
" Sefiperemhesihrahaputchetef is thy name ; Ataream-
" tcherqemturennuparsheta is the name of one of thy
" divine sons, and Panemma that of the other."   And in
yet another chapter [1] the deceased addressing the god
Par says, " Thou art the mighty one of names among
" the gods, the mighty runner whose strides are mighty ;
" thou art the god the mighty one who comest and
" rescuest the needy one and the afflicted from him
" that oppresseth him ; give heed to my cry.   I am
" the Cow, and thy divine name is in my mouth, and
" I will utter it ; Haqahakaher is thy name ; Āuraua-
" aqersaanqrebathi is thy name ; Kherserau is thy
" name ; Kharsatha is thy name.   I praise thy name.
" . . . . O be gracious unto the deceased, and cause
" thou heat to exist under his head, for, indeed, he is
" the soul of the great divine Body which resteth in
" Annu (Heliopolis), whose names are Khukheperuru
" and Barekathatchara."

The examples of the use of names possessing magical
powers described above illustrate the semi-religious

---

[1] See *Chapters of Coming Forth by Day*, p. 289.

views on the subject of names which the Egyptians
held, and we have now to consider briefly the manner in
which the knowledge of a name was employed in uses
less important than those which had for their object
the attainment of life and happiness in the world to
come.   In the famous magical papyrus [1] which Chabas
published [2] we find a series of interesting charms and
magical formulæ which were written to preserve its
possessor from the attacks of sea and river monsters
of every kind, of which the following is an example.
"Hail, lord of the gods! Drive away from me the
"lions of the country of Meru (Meroë?), and the
"crocodiles which come forth from the river, and
"the bite of all poisonous reptiles which crawl forth
"from their holes.   Get thee back, O crocodile Māk,
"thou son of Set! Move not by means of thy tail!
"Work not thy legs and feet! Open not thy mouth!
"Let the water which is before thee turn into a con-
"suming fire, O thou whom the thirty-seven gods did
"make, and whom the serpent of Rā did put in chains,
"O thou who wast fettered with links of iron before
"the boat of Rā! Get thee back, O crocodile Māk,
"thou son of Set!" These words were to be said
over a figure of the god Amen painted on clay; the
god was to have four rams' heads upon one neck, under
his feet was to be a figure of the crocodile Māk, and

---

[1] British Museum, No. 10,042.
[2] *Le Papyrus Magique Harris*, Chalon-sur-Saône, 1860.

to the right and left of him were to be the dog-headed
apes, *i.e.*, the transformed spirits of the dawn, who
sang hymns of praise to Rā when he rose daily.[1]
Again, let us suppose that some water monster wished
to attack a man in a boat. To avoid this the man
stood before the cabin of the boat and, taking a hard
egg in his hand, he said, " O egg of the water which
"hath been spread over the earth, essence of the
"divine apes, the great one in the heaven above and
"in the earth beneath, who dost dwell in the nests
"which are in the waters, I have come forth with thee
"from the water, I have been with thee in thy nest,
" I am Amsu of Coptos, I am Amsu, lord of Kebu."
When he had said these words he would appear to
the animal in the water in the form of the god Amsu,
with whom he had identified himself, and it would be
afraid and flee. At the end of the papyrus in which
the above extracts occur we find a series of magical
names which may be read thus:—Atir-Atisa, Atirkaha-
Atisa, Samumatnatmu-Atisa, Samuanemui-Atisa, Samu-
tekaari-Atisa, Samutekabaiu-Atisa, Samutchakaretcha-
Atisa, Tāuuarehasa, Qina, Hama, Senentuta-Batet-
sataiu, Anrehakatha-sataiu, Haubailra-Haari. From
these and similar magical names it is quite certain that
the Gnostics and other sects which held views akin to
theirs obtained the names which they were so fond of

---

[1] See the scene in the rounded portion of the Metternichstele
illustrated on p. 149.

inscribing upon their amulets and upon the so-called
magical papyri. The last class of documents undoubtedly contains a very large proportion of the
magical ideas, beliefs, formulæ, etc., which were current
in Egypt from the time of the Ptolemies to the end
of the Roman Period, but from about B.C. 150 to A.D.
200 the papyri exhibit traces of the influence of Greek,
Hebrew, and Syrian philosophers and magicians, and
from a passage like the following [1] we may get a proof
of this:—" I call thee, the headless one, that didst
"create earth and heaven, that didst create night and
"day, thee the creator of light and darkness. Thou
" art Osoronnophris, whom no man hath seen at any
"time; thou art Iabas, thou art Iapōs, thou hast dis-
"tinguished the just and the unjust, thou didst make
" female and male, thou didst produce seeds and fruits,
" thou didst make men to love one another and to hate
"one another. I am Moses thy prophet, to whom thou
" didst commit thy mysteries, the ceremonies of Israel;
" thou didst produce the moist and the dry and all
" manner of food. Listen to me: I am an angel of
" Phapro Osoronnophris; this is thy true name, handed
" down to the prophets of Israel. Listen to me.[2] . . ."
In this passage the name Osoronnophris is clearly
a corruption of the old Egyptian names of the

---

[1] See Goodwin, *Fragment of a Græco-Egyptian Work upon Magic*, p. 7.
[2] Here follow a number of names of which Reibet, Athelebersthe,
Blatha, Abeu, Ebenphi, are examples.

great god of the dead "Ausar Unnefer," and Phapro
seems to represent the Egyptian *Per-āa* (literally,
"great house") or "Pharaoh," with the article *pa*
"the" prefixed. It is interesting to note that Moses is
mentioned, a fact which seems to indicate Jewish
influence.

In another magical formula we read,[1] "I call upon
"thee that didst create the earth and bones, and all
"flesh and all spirit, that didst establish the sea and
"that shakest the heavens, that didst divide the light
"from the darkness, the great regulative mind, that
"disposest everything, eye of the world, spirit of spirits,
"god of gods, the lord of spirits, the immoveable Aeon,
"Ιαοουέι, hear my voice. I call upon thee, the ruler of
"the gods, high-thundering Zeus, Zeus, king, Adonai,
"lord, Iaoouêe. I am he that invokes thee in the
"Syrian tongue, the great god, Zaalaêr, Iphphou, do
"thou not disregard the Hebrew appellation Ablana-
"thanalb, Abrasilôa. For I am Silthakhōoukh, Lailam,
"Blasalōth, Iaō, Ieō, Nebouth, Sabiothar, Bōth, Ar-
"bathiaō, Iaoth, Sabaōth, Patoure, Zagourē, Baroukh
"Adonai, Elōai, Iabraam, Barbarauō, Nau, Siph," etc.
The spell ends with the statement that it "loosens
"chains, blinds, brings dreams, creates favour; it may
"be used in common for whatever purpose you will." In
the above we notice at once the use of the seven vowels
which form "a name wherein be contained all Names,

[1] Goodwin, *op. cit.*, p. 21.

" and all Lights, and all Powers." [1] The seven vowels
have, of course, reference to the three vowels " Iaō," [2]
which were intended to represent one of the Hebrew
names for Almighty God, " Jāh." The names " Adonai,
Elōai," are also derived through the Hebrew from the
Bible, and Sabaōth is another well-known Hebrew
word meaning "hosts"; some of the remaining names
could be explained, if space permitted, by Hebrew and
Syriac words. On papyri and amulets the vowels are
written in magical combinations in such a manner as
to form triangles and other shapes; with them are
often found the names of the seven archangels of God;
the following are examples :—

No. 1.[3]   No. 2.[4]   No. 3.[5]

In combination with a number of signs which owe
their origin to the Gnostics the seven vowels were

[1] See Kenyon, *Greek Papyri in the British Museum*, London, 1893, p. 63.

[2] For Iaoouêi we should probably read Iaô ouêi.

[3] British Museum, Gnostic gem, No. G. 33.

[4] Kenyon, *Greek Papyri*, p. 123.

[5] *Ibid.*, p. 123. These names read Michael, Raphael, Gabriel, Souriel, Zaziel, Badakiel, and Suliel.

sometimes engraved upon plaques, or written upon papyri, with the view of giving the possessor power over gods or demons or his fellow creatures. The example printed below is found on a papyrus in the British Museum and accompanies a spell written for the purpose of overcoming the malice of enemies, and for giving security against alarms and nocturnal visions.[1]

Amulet inscribed with signs and letters of magical power for overcoming the malice of enemies. (From Brit. Mus., Greek Papyrus, No. CXXIV.—4th or 5th century.)

But of all the names found upon Gnostic gems two, *i.e.*, Khnoubis (or Khnoumis), and Abrasax (or Abraxas), are of the most frequent occurrence. The first is usually represented as a huge serpent having the head of a lion surrounded by seven or twelve rays. Over the seven rays, one on the point of each, are the seven vowels of the Greek alphabet, which some suppose to

[1] Kenyon, *op. cit.*, p. 121.

refer to the seven heavens; and on the back of the amulet, on which the figure of Khnoumis occurs, is usually found the sign SSS, or the triple S and bar. Khnoumis is, of course, a form of the ancient Egyptian god Khnemu, or "Fashioner" of man and beast, the god to whom many of the attributes of the Creator of the universe were ascribed. Khnemu is, however, often depicted with the head of a ram, and in the later times, as the "beautiful ram of Rā," he has four heads; in the Egyptian monuments he has at times the head of a hawk, but never that of a lion. The god Abrasax is represented in a form which has a human body, the head of a hawk or cock, and legs terminating in serpents; in one hand he holds a knife or dagger, and in the other a shield upon which is inscribed the great name IAω, or JĀH. Considerable difference of opinion exists as to the meaning and derivation of the name Abrasax, but there is no doubt that the god who bore it was a form of the Sun-god, and that he was intended to represent some aspect of the Creator of the world. The name was believed to possess magical powers of the highest class, and Basileides,[1] who gave it currency in the second century, seems to have regarded it as an invincible name. It is probable, however, that its exact meaning was lost at an early date, and that it

[1] He of Alexandria, who lived about A.D. 120. He was a disciple of Menander, and declared that he had received the esoteric doctrine of Saint Peter from Glaucias, a disciple of the Apostle.

soon degenerated into a mere magical symbol, for it is often found inscribed on amulets side by side with scenes and figures with which, seemingly, it cannot have any connexion whatever. Judging from certain Gnostic gems in the British Museum, Abrasax is to be identified with the polytheistic figure that stands in the upper part of the Metternich stele depicted on p. 153. This figure has two bodies, one being that of a man, and the other that of a bird; from these extend four wings, and from each of his knees projects a serpent. He has two pairs of hands and arms; one pair is extended along the wings, each hand holding the symbols of "life," "stability," and "power," and two knives and two serpents; the other pair is pendent, the right hand grasping the sign of life, and the other a sceptre. His face is grotesque, and probably represents that of Bes, or the sun as an old man; on his head is a pylon-shaped object with figures of various animals, and above it a pair of horns which support eight knives and the figure of a god with raised hands and arms, which typifies "millions of years." The god stands upon an oval wherein are depicted figures of various "typhonic" animals, and from each side of his crown proceed several symbols of fire. Whether in the Gnostic system Abraxas absorbed all the names and attributes of this god of many forms cannot be said with certainty.

CHAPTER VI.

MAGICAL CEREMONIES.

IN the preceding pages we have seen how the Egyptians
employed magical stones or amulets, and magical words,
and magical pictures, and magical names, in the performance of deeds both good and evil; it remains to
consider these magical ceremonies in which the skill
of the magician-priest was exerted to its fullest extent,
and with the highest objects, that is to say, to preserve
the human body in a mummified condition, and to
perform the symbolic acts which would restore its
natural functions. When we think of the sublime
character of the life which the souls of the blessed
dead were believed to lead in heaven with the gods,
it is hard to understand why the Egyptians took such
pains to preserve the physical body from decay. No
Egyptian who believed his Scriptures ever expected
that his corruptible body would ascend into heaven
and live with the gods, for they declare in no uncertain
manner that it remains upon the earth whilst the soul
dwells in heaven. But that the preservation of the

body was in some way or for some reason absolutely
necessary is certain, for the art of mummification
flourished for several thousands of years, and unless
there was some good reason, besides the observance of
conservative custom and traditional use, why it should
do so, king and priest, gentle and simple, and rich and
poor, would never have burdened their relatives and
heirs with the expense of costly funeral ceremonies,
and with the performance of rites which were of no avail.
At first sight, too, it seems strange to find the Egyptians
studying carefully how best to provide the dead with
a regular supply of sepulchral offerings, for when we
come to think about it we notice that in arranging for
the well-being of the dead nothing whatever was left
to chance.   For example, a papyrus will contain several
prayers and pictures with appropriate formulæ, the
object of each of which is to give the deceased meat
and drink ; any one of these would have been enough
for the purpose, but it was thought best in such an
important matter to make assurance doubly sure, and
if there was the least doubt about the efficacy of one
Chapter one or more of the same class were added.
Similarly, the tendency of the natural body after death
being to decay, the greatest care was taken in mummi-
fying its various members, lest perchance any one of
them should be neglected accidentally, and should,
either by the omission of the words of power that
ought to have been said over it, or through the lax

performance of some ceremony, decay and perish. The Egyptian declared that he was immortal, and believed that he would enjoy eternal life in a spiritual body; yet he attempted by the performance of magical ceremonies and the recital of words of power to make his corruptible body to endure for ever. He believed that he would feed upon the celestial and imperishable food whereon the gods lived, but at the same time he spared no effort or expense to provide for his tomb being supplied at stated intervals throughout the year with perishable food in the shape of offerings of oxen, feathered fowl, cakes, bread, and the like. He mummified his dead and swathed them in linen bandages, and then by the performance of magical ceremonies and by the recital of words of power sought to give back to their members the strength to eat, and drink, and talk, and think, and move at will. Indeed, all the evidence now forthcoming seems to prove that he never succeeded in bringing himself to think that the gods could do without his help, or that the pictures or representations of the scenes which took place in the life, and death, and burial, and resurrection of Osiris, upon which he relied so implicitly, could possibly fail to be as efficacious as the actual power of the god himself.

The examination of mummies has shown us with tolerable clearness what methods were adopted in preparing bodies for bandaging and final ornamentation,

and the means adopted for disposing of the more
corruptible portions of the body are well known from
classical and other writers.   But for an account of the
manner in which the body was bandaged, and a list of
the unguents and other materials employed in the process, and the words of power which were spoken as
each bandage was laid in its place, we must have
recourse to a very interesting papyrus which has been
edited and translated by M. Maspero under the title of
Le Rituel de l'Embaumement.[1]   The first part of the
papyrus, which probably gave instructions for the
evisceration of the body, is wanting, and only the
section which refers to the bandaging is at all perfect.
The text opens with an address to the deceased in
which it is said, " The perfume of Arabia hath been
" brought to thee to make perfect thy smell through
" the scent of the god.   Here are brought to thee
" liquids which have come forth from Rā to make
" perfect . . . thy smell in the Hall [of Judgment].
" O sweet-smelling soul of the great god, thou dost
" contain such a sweet odour that thy face shall neither
" change nor perish. . . . Thy members shall become
" young in Arabia, and thy soul shall appear over thy
" body in Ta-neter (*i.e.*, the ' divine land ')."   After this
the priest or mummifier was to take a vase of liquid
which contained ten perfumes, and to smear therewith
the body from head to foot twice, taking especial care

[1] In *Mémoire sur quelques Papyrus du Louvre*, Paris, 1875.

to anoint the head thoroughly. He was then to say, " Osiris (*i.e.*, the deceased), thou hast received the per- " fume which shall make thy members perfect. Thou " receivest the source [of life] and thou takest the form " of the great Disk (*i.e.*, Aten), which uniteth itself unto " thee to give enduring form to thy members; thou " shalt unite with Osiris in the great Hall. The " unguent cometh unto thee to fashion thy members " and to gladden thy heart, and thou shalt appear in the " form of Rā; it shall make thee to be sound when thou " settest in the sky at eventide, and it shall spread " abroad the smell of thee in the nomes of Aqert. . . . " Thou receivest the oil of the cedar in Amentet, and " the cedar which came forth from Osiris cometh unto " thee; it delivereth thee from thy enemies, and it pro- " tecteth thee in the nomes. Thy soul alighteth upon " the venerable sycamores. Thou criest to Isis, and " Osiris heareth thy voice, and Anubis cometh unto " thee to invoke thee. Thou receivest the oil of the " country of Manu which hath come from the East, and " Rā riseth upon thee at the gates of the horizon, at the " holy doors of Neith. Thou goest therein, thy soul is " in the upper heaven, and thy body is in the lower " heaven . . . O Osiris, may the Eye of Horus cause " that which floweth forth from it to come to thee, and " to thy heart for ever!" These words having been said, the whole ceremony was repeated, and then the internal organs which had been removed from the body

were placed in the "liquid of the children of Horus,"
so that the liquid of this god might enter into them,
and whilst they were being thus treated a chapter was
read over them and they were put in the funeral chest.
When this was done the internal organs were placed on
the body, and the body having been made to lie straight
the backbone was immersed in holy oil, and the face of
the deceased was turned towards the sky; the bandage
of Sebek and Sedi was then laid upon the backbone.
In a long speech the deceased is addressed and told
that the liquid is "secret," and that it is an emanation
of the gods Shu and Seb, and that the resin of Phœnicia
and the bitumen of Byblos will make his burial perfect
in the underworld, and give him his legs, and facilitate
his movements, and sanctify his steps in the Hall of
Seb. Next gold, silver, lapis-lazuli, and turquoise are
brought to the deceased, and crystal to lighten his face,
and carnelian to strengthen his steps; these form
amulets which will secure for him a free passage in the
underworld. Meanwhile the backbone is kept in oil,
and the face of the deceased is turned towards the
heavens; and next the gilding of the nails of the fingers
and toes begins. When this has been done, and
portions of the fingers have been wrapped in linen
made at Saïs, the following address is made to the
deceased:—" O Osiris, thou receivest thy nails of gold,
"thy fingers of gold, and thy thumb of *smu* (or *uasm*)
"metal; the liquid of Rā entereth into thee as well

"as into the divine members of Osiris, and thou
"journeyest on thy legs to the immortal abode. Thou
"hast carried thy hands to the house of eternity, thou
"art made perfect in gold, thou dost shine brightly in
"*smu* metal, and thy fingers shine in the dwelling of
"Osiris, in the sanctuary of Horus himself. O Osiris,
"the gold of the mountains cometh to thee; it is a holy
"talisman of the gods in their abodes, and it lighteneth
"thy face in the lower heaven. Thou breathest in
"gold, thou appearest in *smu* metal, and the dwellers
"in Re-stau receive thee; those who are in the funeral
"chest rejoice because thou hast transformed thyself
"into a hawk of gold by means of thy amulets (*or*
"talismans) of the City of Gold," etc. When these
words have been said, a priest who is made to personify
Anubis comes to the deceased and performs certain
symbolical ceremonies by his head, and lays certain
bandages upon it. When the head and mouth and face
have been well oiled the bandage of Nekheb is laid on
the forehead, the bandage of Hathor on the face, the
bandage of Thoth upon the two ears, and the bandage
of Nebt-hetep on the nape of the neck. Over the head
was laid the bandage of Sekhet, in two pieces, and over
each ear, and each nostril, and each cheek was fastened
a bandage or strip of linen; over the forehead went
four pieces of linen, on the top of the head two, outside
the mouth two, and inside two, over the chin two, and
over the nape of the neck four large pieces; there were

to be twenty-two pieces to the right and to the left of
the face passing over the two ears. The Lady of the
West is then addressed in these words:—" Grant thou
" that breathing may take place in the head of the
" deceased in the underworld, and that he may see with
" his eyes, and that he may hear with his two ears;
" and that he may breathe through his nose; and that
" he may be able to utter sounds with his mouth; and
" that he may be able to speak with his tongue in the
" underworld. Receive thou his voice in the Hall of
" Maāti and his speech in the Hall of Seb in the
" presence of the Great God, the lord of Amentet."
The addresses which follow these words have reference
to the delights and pleasures of the future life which
shall be secured for him through the oil and unguents,
which are duly specified and described, and through the
magical figures which are drawn upon the bandages.
The protecting properties of the turquoise and other
precious stones are alluded to, and after a further
anointing with oil and the placing of grains of myrrh
and resin, the deceased is declared to have " received
" his head," and he is promised that it shall nevermore
depart from him. On the conclusion of the ceremonies
which concern the head the deceased has the power to
go in among the holy and perfect spirits, his name is
exalted among men, the denizens of heaven receive his
soul, the beings of the underworld bow down before his
body, the dwellers upon earth adore him, and the

o

inhabitants of the funeral mountain renew for him his youth. Besides these things, Anubis and Horus make perfect his bandages, and the god Thoth protects his members by his words of magical power; and he himself has learned the magical formulæ which are necessary to make his path straight in the underworld, and also the proper way in which to utter them. All these benefits were secured for him by the use of bandages and unguents which possess both magical names and properties, and by the words of power uttered by the priests who recited the Ritual of Embalmment, and by the ceremonies which the priest who personated Anubis performed beside the body of the deceased in imitation of those which the god Anubis performed for the dead god Osiris in remote days.

Next the left hand of the deceased was mummified and bandaged according to the instructions given in the Ritual of Embalmment. The hand was stretched out on a piece of linen, and a ring was passed over the fingers; it was then filled with thirty-six of the substances which were used in embalming, according to the number of the forms of the god Osiris. This done, the hand was bandaged with a strip of linen in six folds, upon which were drawn figures of Isis and Hāpi. The right hand was treated in a similar way, only the figures drawn upon the bandages were those of Rā and Amsu; and when the appropriate words had been

recited over both hands divine protection was assured
them. After these things the ceremonies concerning
the right and left arms were performed, and these were
followed by rubbing the soles of the feet and the legs
and the thighs, first with black-stone oil, and secondly
with holy oil. The toes were wrapped in linen, and
a piece of linen was laid on each leg; on each piece
was drawn the figure of a jackal, that on the right leg
representing Anubis, and that on the left Horus. When
flowers of the ānkham plant and other substances had
been laid beside and on the legs, and they had been
treated with ebony-gum water and holy oil, and appropriate addresses had been said, the ceremony of
bandaging the body was ended. Everything that could
be done to preserve the body was now done, and every
member of it was, by means of the words of power
which changed perishable substances into imperishable,
protected to all eternity; when the final covering of
purple or white linen had been fastened upon it, the
body was ready for the tomb.

But the Ritual of Embalmment which has been
briefly described above seems to belong to a late period
of Egyptian history, and although the ideas and beliefs
contained in it are as old as Egyptian civilization itself,
it seems as if it was intended to take the place of a
much older and more elaborate work which was in
use as far back as the period in which the Great
Pyramid was built, and which was intended to be

recited during the performance of a complex series of
ceremonies, some of which are still not completely
understood.   It seems as if the performance of all the
ceremonies would require several days, and it is clear
that only the wealthy could afford the expense which
must have attended such elaborate obsequies; for the
poorer classes of men the various ceremonies must have
been greatly curtailed, and at a very early period we
find that a shortened form of ritual had taken their
place.   Of all the ceremonies, the most important was
that of the "Opening of the Mouth and Eyes," which
was performed either on the mummy itself or upon a
statue which represented it.   It has already been stated
that the Egyptians believed that they could transmit
to a statue the attributes of the person in whose image
it was made, and similarly that that which was done to
the statue of the mummified person was also done to it.
The use of a statue instead of the actual mummy has
obvious advantages, for the ceremony could be performed at any time and in any place, and the presence
of the mummy was unnecessary.   As a matter of fact
the ceremony was performed in a chamber at the
entrance to the tomb, or outside the tomb at a place
which had been made ceremonially pure or consecrated,
and those who took part in it were :—(1) The *Kher-heb*,
or chief officiating priest, who held a roll of papyrus
in his hand.   (2) The *Sem* priest.   (3) The *Smer*, who
was, perhaps, some intimate friend of the deceased.

(4) The *Sa-mer-ef*,[1] or man who was either the son of the deceased or his representative. (5) The *Tcherau-ur*, or woman who represented Isis. (6) The *Tcherau-sheraut*, or woman who represented Nephthys. (7) The *Menhu*, or slaughterer. (8) The *Am-asi* priest. (9) The *Am-khent* priest. (10) A number of people who represented the armed guard of Horus. All these became actors in scenes which were intended to represent the events which took place in connexion with the burial of Osiris, with whom the deceased is now identified; the two women took the parts of the goddesses Isis and Nephthys, and the men those of the gods who helped them in the performance of their pious duties. From the scenes[2] which accompany the texts[3] relating to the ceremony of opening the mouth and eyes we see that it began with the sprinkling of water round about the statue or mummy from four vessels, one for each quarter of the earth, and with the recital of addresses to the gods Horus, Set, Thoth, and Sept; this act restored to the deceased the use of his head. The sprinkling of water was followed by a purification by means of incense, also contained in four vases, one for each of the four quarters of the earth. The burning

---

.[1] *I.e.*, " the son who loveth him."

[2] See Dümichen, *Der Grabpalast des Patuamenap*, Leipzig, vol. i., 1884; vol. ii., 1885; vol. iii., 1894; and Champollion, *Monuments*, Paris, 1845, tom. iii., plates 243-248.

[3] See Schiaparelli, *Il Libro dei Funerali degli antichi Egiziani*, Turin, 1882; see also Maspero, *Le Rituel du sacrifice funéraire* (*Revue de l'Histoire des Religions*, tom. xv., p. 159 ff.).

of this sweet-smelling substance assisted in opening the mouth of the deceased and in strengthening his heart. At this stage the *Sem* priest dressed himself in the skin of a cow, and lying down upon a kind of couch pretended to be asleep; but he was roused up by the *Am-asi* priest in the presence of the *Kher-heb* and the *Am-khent* priest, and when the *Sem* priest had seated himself upon a seat, the four men together represented the four children of Horus,[1] or the gods with the heads of a hawk, an ape, a jackal, and a man respectively. The *Sem* priest then said, " I have seen my father in " all his forms," which the other men in turn repeat. The meaning of this portion of the ceremony is hard to explain, but M. Maspero [2] thinks that it was intended to bring back to the body of the deceased its shadow (*khaibit*), which had departed from it when it died. The preliminary purifications being ended, and the shadow having been joined to the body once more, the statue or mummy is approached by the men who represent the armed guard of Horus; and one of their number, having taken upon himself the character of Horus, the son of Osiris and Isis, touches its mouth with his finger. The *Kher-heb* next made ready to perform the sacrifice which was intended to commemorate the slaughter, at some very early period, of the fiends who were the friends of Set. It seems that,

---

[1] *I.e.*, Mestha, Hāpi, Tuamutef and Qebhsennuf.
[2] *Op. cit.*, p. 168.

the soul of Horus dwelt in an eye, and that Set nearly
succeeded in devouring it; but Horus vanquished Set
and saved his eye. Set's associates then changed themselves into the forms of animals, and birds, and fish,
but they were caught, and their heads were cut off;
Set, however, who was concealed in the form of a pig,
contrived to escape. The sacrifice consisted of a bull
(or cow) or two, two gazelles or antelopes, and ducks.
When the bull had been slain, one of the forelegs was
cut off, and the heart taken out, and offered to the
statue or mummy; the *Sem* priest then took the bleed-
ing leg and touched, or pretended to touch, the mouth
and eyes with it four times. The slaughtered gazelles
or antelopes and ducks were simply offered before the
statue. The *Sem* priest next said to the statue, "I
"have come to embrace thee, I am thy son Horus, I
"have pressed thy mouth; I am thy son, I love thee.
". . . Thy mouth was closed, but I have set in order
"for thee thy mouth and thy teeth." He then brought
two instruments, ⌢, called "Seb-ur" and "Tuntet"
respectively, and touched the mouth of the statue or
mummy with them, whilst the *Kher-heb* said, "Thy
"mouth was closed, but I have set in order for thee
"thy mouth and thy teeth. I open for thee thy mouth,
"I open for thee thy two eyes. I have opened for thee
"thy mouth with the instrument of Anubis. I have
"opened thy mouth with the instrument of Anubis,
"with the iron implement with which the mouths of the

"gods were opened.   Horus, open the mouth!   Horus,
"open the mouth!   Horus hath opened the mouth
"of the dead, as he in times of old opened the mouth of
"Osiris, with the iron which came forth from Set, with
"the iron instrument with which he opened the mouths
"of the gods.   He hath opened thy mouth with it.   The
"deceased shall walk and shall speak, and his body
"shall be with the great company of the gods in the
"Great House of the Aged One in Annu, and he shall
"receive there the *ureret* crown from Horus, the lord
"of mankind."   Thus the mouth and the eyes of the
deceased are opened.   The *Sem* priest then took in
his hand the instrument called *ur hekau*, *i.e.*, the
"mighty one of enchantments," a curious, sinuous
piece of wood, one end of which is in the form of a
ram's head surmounted by a uraeus, and touched the
mouth and the eyes of the statue or mummy four
times, whilst the *Kher-heb* recited a long address in
which he declared that this portion of the ceremony
had secured for the deceased all the benefits which
accrued to the god Osiris from the actions of Nut,
Horus, and Set, when he was in a similar state.   It
has been said above that every dead man hoped to
be provided with the *hekau*, or words of power, which
were necessary for him in the next world, but without
a mouth it was impossible for him to utter them.
Now that the mouth, or rather the use of it, was
restored to the deceased, it was all important to give

him not only the words of power, but also the ability
to utter them correctly and in such wise that the
gods and other beings would hearken to them and
obey them ; four touches of the *ur hekau* instrument
on the lips endowed the deceased with the faculty
of uttering the proper words in the proper manner in
each of the four quarters of the world. When this
had been done, several other ceremonies were performed with the object of allowing the "son who
"loveth him" or his representative to take part in the
opening of the mouth of his father. In order to do
this he took in his hand a metal chisel and touched
the openings of the mouth and of the eyes, and then
the *Sem* priest touched them first with his little finger,
and afterwards with a little bag filled with pieces
of red stone or carnelian, with the idea, M. Maspero
thinks, of restoring to the lips and eyelids the colour
which they had lost during the process of mummification. The "son who loves him" then took four
objects called "iron of the South, and iron of the
"North," and laid each of them four times upon
the mouth and the eyes while the *Kher-heb* recited
the proper address in which the mummy or statue
is said to have had his mouth and lips established
firmly. This done, the *Sem* priest brings an instrument
called the "Pesh-en-kef," Υ, and touches the mouth
of the mummy or statue therewith, and says, "O
"Osiris, I have stablished for thee the two jaw-bones

"in thy face, and they are now separated"; that is to say, the bandages with which they have been tied up can no longer prevent their movement when the deceased wishes to eat. After the Pesh-en-kef had been used the *Sem* priest brought forward a basket or vessel of some kind of food in the shape of balls, and by the order of the *Kher-heb* offered them to the mouth of the mummy, and when this portion of the ceremony was ended, the *Sem* priest took an ostrich feather, and waved it before its face four times, but with what object is not clear. Such are the ceremonies which it was thought necessary to perform in order to restore to the deceased the functions which his body possessed upon earth. But it must be remembered that hitherto only the "bull of the south" has been sacrificed, and that the "bull of the north" has yet to be offered up; and all the ceremonies which have been already performed must be repeated if the deceased would have the power to go forth at will over the whole earth. From the earliest times the South and the North were the two great sections into which the world was divided, and each section possessed its own special gods, all of whom had to be propitiated by the deceased; hence most religious ceremonies were ordered to be performed in duplicate. In later days each section was divided into two parts, and the four divisions thus made were apportioned to the four children of Horus; hence prayers and formulæ

The ceremony of "opening the mouth" being performed on the mummy of Hunefer, about B.C. 1350. (From the *Papyrus of Hunefer*, sheet 5.)

were usually said four times, once in honour of each god, and the rubrical directions on this point are definite.

In the limited space of this book it is not possible to reproduce all the scenes of the ceremony of opening the mouth and the eyes which are depicted in the tombs and elsewhere, but on page 199 is a general view of the ceremony as it is often given in the papyri of the XVIIIth and XIXth dynasties. On the right we see the pyramidal tomb in the Theban hill with its open door, and by the side of it is the funeral stele with a rounded top inscribed with a figure of the deceased standing in adoration before Osiris, and with a prayer to the god for sepulchral offerings. Anubis, the god of the dead, embraces the mummy, thus indicating his readiness to take the deceased under his protection. Nasha, the wife of the deceased, stands weeping before the mummy, and at his feet kneels another weeping woman, probably his daughter. Anubis and the mummy stand upon a layer of sand which has been placed there with the object of sanctifying the ground. A priest clad in a panther's skin holds a censer containing burning incense in one hand, and a vase, from which he sprinkles water, in the other. One ministrant holds the two instruments "Tun-tet" and "Seb-ur" in the right hand, and the "Ur hekau" instrument in the left; and another offers four vases of unguent. In the lower register are a cow and her

calf, and two men are carrying along to the mummy
the haunch which we must assume to have been
recently cut from the slaughtered bull, and the heart
which has just been taken out of him. On a table
we see lying a number of objects, the "Meskhet," and
"Pesh-en-kef," and other instruments, two sets of four
vases for holding unguents and oil, the bags of colour,
the iron of the south and north, etc. The text which
runs in short vertical lines above the scene reads:—
"The Chapter of the opening of the mouth of the
"statue of Osiris, the royal scribe, Hunefer, which is
"to be performed [when] its face [looketh] towards the
"south, [and when it is set] upon the sand behind
"him. And the Kher-heb shall say four times unto
"the *Sem* priest as he goeth round about him bearing
"four vases of water : 'Thou art pure with the purifi-
"cation of Horus, and Horus is pure with thy purifica-
"tion. Thou art pure with the purification of Thoth,
"and Thoth is pure with thy purification. Thou art
"pure with the purification of Sep, and Sep is pure
"with thy purification. Thou art pure with the puri-
"fication of Seb, and Seb is pure with thy purification.
"Pure. Pure.' [Say] four times. 'Incense hath been
"offered unto thee of the incense of Horus, and incense
"hath been offered unto Horus of thy incense. Incense
"hath been offered unto thee of the incense of Thoth,
"and incense hath been offered unto Thoth of thy
"incense. Incense hath been offered unto thee of

"the incense of Sep, and incense hath been offered "unto Sep of thy incense. Incense hath been offered "unto thee of the incense of Seb, and incense hath "been offered unto Seb of thy incense.'" The above words are all the text that the scribe considered it necessary to give in the Papyrus of Hunefer, and that he curtailed the representation of the ceremony of opening the mouth and eyes as much as possible is evident.

The performance of the ceremony of opening the mouth was followed by a number of other less important ceremonies which had for their object the providing of the mummy or statue with scents, and unguents, and various articles of wearing apparel; these were not essentials, but sufficient importance was attached to them to make the performance of them almost obliga- tory. Among the objects presented to the deceased in these ceremonies scents and perfumed unguents play a prominent part, and this is not to be wondered at. To certain kinds of oil, magical properties have been attached from time immemorial in the East, and the important place which they occupied in the ceremonies and rituals of many nations proves that remark- able effects were expected to follow their use. The living made use of oil to soften the skin and to pre- serve it from the parching heat of the sun, and the dead were anointed with it during the process of mummification so that their skins might, through the magical words which were pronounced whilst it was being rubbed on them, remain soft for all time, and so that the curative properties of the oil might heal the wounds which the mummifiers had made. A glance at the medical papyri of Egypt will shew that oil appears in scores of prescriptions, and it was no less useful to the magician[1] than to the physician in producing good or evil results. It seems to have been used with the idea of effecting transformations by the former, just as it was employed by the priest in the performance of certain important religious ceremonies, and a curious survival of this use is mentioned by Lucian,[2] who relates that a woman transformed herself into a night-raven by its means. The woman first undressed herself, and going to a lamp threw two grains of incense into the flame and recited certain words ; she then went to a large chest containing several bottles, and taking out one which, the writer thinks, contained oil, rubbed all her body with the liquid, from head to foot, beginning with the ends of the nails, and suddenly feathers and wings began to grow upon her, and a hooked, horny beak took the place of her nose. In a very short time she resembled a bird in every respect, and when she saw that she was well feathered, she flew upwards and, uttering the cry of a night-

---

[1] See the description of the ceremony of the beetle, p. 42.

[2] *Lucius sive Asinus*, xlii., 12 (ed. Didot, p. 449).   Compare also § 54 (p. 466).

raven, disappeared through the window.[1]   In connexion
with the recital of certain Chapters of the Book of the
Dead a number of interesting ceremonies were performed, but as they only illustrate the beliefs described
above they need not be mentioned here.

[1] From the words, χρίσματι μεμαγευμένῳ ἐπαλείψασα ὄνον ποιήσειε
(see *Lucius sive Asinus*, xlii., 54, ed. Didot, p. 466), it is clear that the
person who is speaking believed that he had been transformed into
an ass by means of the use of " bewitched oil."

P

CHAPTER VII.

DEMONIACAL POSSESSION, DREAMS, GHOSTS, LUCKY AND
UNLUCKY DAYS, HOROSCOPES, PROGNOSTICATIONS,
TRANSFORMATIONS, AND THE WORSHIP OF ANIMALS.

THE Egyptians, in common with many other Eastern
nations, believed that certain sicknesses and diseases
might be cured by certain medicaments pure and
simple, but that others needed not only drugs but the
recital of words of power to effect their cure. There
is good reason for thinking that some diseases were
attributed to the action of evil spirits or demons, which
had the power of entering into human bodies and of
vexing them in proportion to their malignant nature
and influence,[1] but the texts do not afford much information on the matter. Incidentally, however, we have
one interesting proof that foreign peoples believed that
the Egyptians were able to cure the diseases caused by
demoniacal possession, and the exercise of their power

[1] As recently as 1895 this belief existed in Ireland, for according
to the *Times* of April 2, 3, 6, and 8, Michael Cleary was charged on
April 1 at Clonmel with having, on March 14, burnt his wife Bridget,
aged 27, for being a witch, thus causing her death, at Baltyvadhen,

on the occasion described was considered to be so noteworthy that the narrative of it was inscribed upon a stele[1] and set up in the temple[2] of the god Khonsu at Thebes, so that all men might read and know what a marvellous cure his priests had effected. It appears that king Rameses II. was in Mesopotamia " according " to his wont, year by year," and all the chiefs of the countries round about came to pay their respects to him, and they sought to obtain his goodwill and protection, probably even an alliance, by bringing to him gifts of gold, and lapis-lazuli, and turquoise, and of every kind of valuable thing which the land produced,

county Tipperary. Johanna Burke swore that boiling herbs out of a saucepan on the fire were forced down the throat of the deceased, her husband asking her in the name of the Father, Son, and Holy Ghost, if she was his wife. He then stripped her naked, threw her on the floor, and pouring paraffin over her, set her on fire. Cleary, assisted by J. Dunne, P. Kennedy, W. Kennedy, and others, next took her to the fire and forced her to sit upon it in order to " drive " out the witch " which possessed her. She was next laid upon the bed and shaken, while her husband recited the words " Away with you," meaning the evil spirit, or spirits, and at six o'clock on the morning of the 15th of March the priest was sent for to exorcise the spirits with which the house was thought to be filled. A herbalist called Denis Ganey was present at the time, being charged as an accessory before the fact. The prisoners were found guilty and were sentenced to terms of imprisonment as follows:—M. Cleary 20 years, J. Dunne 3 years, P. Kennedy 5 years, W. Kennedy 18 months, J. Kennedy 18 months, Boland Kennedy 6 months, Michael Kennedy 6 months.

[1] Originally published by Prisse, *Monuments Égyptiens*, Paris, 1817, pl. 24.

[2] It is now preserved in the Bibliothèque Nationale at Paris; for a full description and translation of it see E. de Rougé, *Étude sur une stèle Égyptienne*, Paris, 1858.

and every man sought to outdo his neighbour by
the lavishness of his gifts. Among others there came
the Prince of Bekhten, and at the head of all the
offerings which he presented to His Majesty he placed
his eldest daughter, who was very beautiful. When
the king saw her he thought her the most beautiful
girl he had ever seen, and he bestowed upon her the
title of "Royal spouse, chief lady, Rā-neferu" (i.e., "the
"beauties of Rā," the Sun-god), and took her to Egypt;
and when they arrived in that country the king married
her. One day during the fifteenth year of the king's
reign, when His Majesty was in Thebes celebrating
the festival of Amen-Rā, a messenger came to the king
and reported the arrival of an ambassador from the
Prince of Bekhten who had brought rich gifts for the
royal lady Rā-neferu. When he had been led into
the king's presence, he did homage before him, saying,
"Glory and praise be unto thee, O thou Sun of the
"nations; grant that we may live before thee!"
Having said these words he bowed down and touched
the ground with his head three times, and said, " I
"have come unto thee, O my sovereign Lord, on behalf
"of the lady Bent-ent-resht, the younger sister of the
"royal spouse Rā-neferu, for, behold, an evil disease
"hath laid hold upon her body ; I beseech thy Majesty
"to send a physician [1] to see her." Then the king
straightway ordered the books of the "double house

---

[1] *Rekh khet*, " knower of things."

Stele recording the casting out of the devil from the Princess of Bekhten. On the right the king is offering incense to Khonsu Nefer-hetep, and on the left a priest is offering incense to Khonsu, "the great god who driveth away devils." (From Prisse, *Monuments*, plate 24.)

"of life" to be brought and the learned men to appear, and when they had come into his presence he ordered them to choose from among their number a man "wise "of heart and cunning of finger," that he might send him to Bekhten; they did so, and their choice fell upon one Tehuti-em-heb. This sage having come before the king was ordered to set out for Bekhten in company with the ambassador, and he departed; and when they had arrived there the Egyptian priest found the lady Bent-ent-resht to be possessed of a demon or spirit over which he was powerless. The Prince of Bekhten, seeing that the priest was unable to afford relief to his daughter, sent once. again to the king, and entreated him to send a god to his help.

When the ambassador from Bekhten arrived in Egypt the king was in Thebes, and on hearing what was asked he went into the temple of Khonsu Nefer-hetep, and besought that god to allow his counterpart Khonsu to depart to Bekhten and to deliver the daughter of the prince of that country from the power of the demon that possessed her. It seems as if the sage Tehuti-em-heb had been sent to Bekhten by the advice of the god, for the king says, in addressing the god, "I have come once again into thy presence"; but in any case Khonsu Nefer-hetep agreed to his request, and a fourfold measure of magical power was imparted to the statue of the god which was to go to Bekhten. The god, seated in his boat, and five other boats with figures of gods in them, accompanied by chariots and horses on the right hand and on the left, set out from Egypt, and after travelling for seventeen months arrived in Bekhten, where they were received with great honour. The god Khonsu went to the place where Bent-ent-resht was, and, having performed a magical ceremony over her, the demon departed from her and she was cured straightway. Then the demon addressed the Egyptian god, saying, " Grateful and " welcome is thy coming unto us, O great god, thou " vanquisher of the hosts of darkness! Bekhten is " thy city, the inhabitants thereof are thy slaves, and " I am thy servant; and I will depart unto the place " whence I came that I may gratify thee, for unto this " end hast thou come thither. And I beseech thy " Majesty to command that the Prince of Bekhten and " I may hold a festival together." To the demon's request Khonsu agreed, and he commanded his priest to tell the Prince of Bekhten to make a great festival in honour of the demon; this having been done by the command of Khonsu the demon departed to his own place.

When the Prince of Bekhten saw that Khonsu was thus powerful, he and all his people rejoiced exceedingly, and he determined that the god should not be allowed to return to Egypt, and as a result Khonsu remained in Bekhten for three years, four months, and five days. On a certain day, however, the Prince was

sleeping, and he dreamed a dream in which he saw the
god Khonsu come forth from his shrine in the form of
a hawk of gold, and having mounted into the air he
flew away to Egypt. The Prince woke up in a state of
great perturbation, and having inquired of the Egyptian
priest was told by him that the god had departed to
Egypt, and that his chariot must now be sent back.
Then the Prince gave to Khonsu great gifts, and they
were taken to Egypt and laid before the god Khonsu
Nefer-hetep in his temple at Thebes. In early
Christian literatures we find a number of examples of
demoniacal possession in which the demon who has
entered the body yields it up before a demon of greater
power than himself, but the demon who is expelled is
invariably hostile to him that expels him, and he
departs from before him with every sign of wrath and
shame. The fact that it was believed possible for the
demon of Bekhten and the god Khonsu to fraternize,
and to be present together at a festival made by the
Prince of the country, shews that the people of Bekhten
ascribed the same attributes to spirits or demons as
they did to men. The demon who possessed the
princess recognized in Khonsu a being who was
mightier than himself, and, like a vanquished king, he
wished to make the best terms he could with his
conqueror, and to be on good terms with him.

The Egyptians believed that the divine powers
frequently made known their will to them by means of

dreams, and they attached considerable importance to
them ; the figures of the gods and the scenes which they
saw when dreaming seemed to them to prove the existence of another world which was not greatly unlike that
already known to them.   The knowledge of the art of
procuring dreams and the skill to interpret them were
greatly prized in Egypt as elsewhere in the East, and
the priest or official who possessed such gifts sometimes
rose to places of high honour in the state, as we may
see from the example of Joseph,[1] for it was universally
believed that glimpses of the future were revealed to
man in dreams.   As instances of dreams recorded in the
Egyptian texts may be quoted those of Thothmes IV.,
king of Egypt about B.C. 1450, and Nut-Amen,
king of the Eastern Sûdân and Egypt, about B.C. 670.
A prince, according to the stele which he set up before
the breast of the Sphinx at Gîzeh, was one day hunting
near this emblem of Râ-Harmachis, and he sat down to
rest under its shadow and fell asleep and dreamed a
dream.   In it the god appeared to him, and, having
declared that he was the god Harmachis-Khepera-Râ-
Temu, promised him that if he would clear away from
the Sphinx, his own image, the drift sand in which it
was becoming buried, he would give to him the sovereignty of the lands of the South and of the North, *i.e.,*
of all Egypt.   In due course the prince became king
of Egypt under the title of Thothmes IV., and the stele

---

[1] See Genesis, Chapters xl., xli.

which is dated on the 19th day of the month Hathor
of the first year of Thothmes IV. proves that the royal
dreamer carried out the wishes of the god.[1] Of Nut-
Amen, the successor of the great Piānkhi who came
down from Gebel Barkal and conquered all Egypt from
Syenè to the sea, we read that in the first year of his
reign he one night dreamed a dream wherein he saw
two serpents, one on his right hand and the other on
his left; when he awoke they had disappeared.
Having asked for an interpretation of the dream he was
told :—" The land of the South is thine, and thou shalt
" have dominion over the land of the North : the White
" Crown and the Red Crown shall adorn thy head.
" The length and the breadth of the land shall be given
" unto thee, and the god Amen, the only god, shall be
" with thee." [2] The two serpents were the symbols of
the goddesses Nekhebet and Uatchet, the mistresses
of the South and North respectively. As the result of
his dream Nut-Amen invaded Egypt successfully and
brought back much spoil, a portion of which he dedi-
cated to the service of his god Amen.

Since dreams and visions in which the future might
be revealed to the sleeper were greatly desired, the
Egyptian magician set himself to procure such for his
clients by various devices, such as drawing magical
pictures and reciting magical words. The following

[1] See Vyse, *Appendix*, London, 1842, vol. iii., p. 114 ff.
[2] See Brugsch, *Egypt under the Pharaohs*, vol. ii., p. 259.

are examples of spells for procuring a vision and dreams,
taken from British Museum Papyrus, No. 122, lines
64 ff. and 359 ff.[1]

"To obtain a vision from [the god] Bes. Make a
"drawing of Besa, as shewn below, on your left hand,
"and envelope your hand in a strip of black cloth that
"has been consecrated to Isis (?) and lie down to sleep
"without speaking a word, even in answer to a question.
"Wind the remainder of the cloth round your neck.
"The ink with which you write must be composed of
"the blood of a cow, the blood of a white dove, fresh (?)
"frankincense, myrrh, black writing-ink, cinnabar,
"mulberry juice, rain-water, and the juice of worm-
"wood and vetch. With this write your petition before
"the setting sun, [saying], 'Send the truthful seer out
"of the holy shrine, I beseech thee, Lampsuer, Sumarta,
"Baribas, Dardalam, Iorlex: O Lord send the sacred
"deity Anuth, Anuth, Salbana, Chambré, Breïth, now,
"now, quickly, quickly. Come in this very night.'"[2]

"To procure dreams: Take a clean linen bag and
"write upon it the names given below. Fold it up and
"make it into a lamp-wick, and set it alight, pouring
"pure oil over it. The word to be written is this:
"'Armiuth, Lailamchoüch, Arsenophrephren, Phtha,
"Archentechtha.' Then in the evening, when you are

---

[1] See *Catalogue of Greek Papyri*, vol. i. p. 118.

[2] A sketch of the god Besa is given at the end of the papyrus.
See the description of the "Metternichstele" above, p. 147 ff.

"going to bed, which you must do without touching food
" [or, pure from all defilement], do thus. Approach the
"lamp and repeat seven times the formula given below:
"then extinguish it and lie down to sleep. The
"formula is this: ' Sachmu . . . epaëma Ligotereënch:
"the Aeon, the Thunderer, Thou that hast swallowed
" the snake and dost exhaust the moon, and dost raise
" up the orb of the sun in his season, Chthetho is thy
"name; I require, O lords of the gods, Seth, Chreps,
"give me the information that I desire.'"

The peculiar ideas which the Egyptians held about
the composition of man greatly favoured the belief in
apparitions and ghosts. According to them a man
consisted of a physical body, a shadow, a double, a soul,
a heart, a spirit called the *khu*, a power, a name, and
a spiritual body. When the body died the shadow
departed from it, and could only be brought back to it
by the performance of a mystical ceremony; the double
lived in the tomb with the body, and was there visited
by the soul whose habitation was in heaven. The soul
was, from one aspect, a material thing, and like the *ka*,
or double, was believed to partake of the funeral offerings which were brought to the tomb; one of the chief
objects of sepulchral offerings of meat and drink was
to keep the double in the tomb and to do away with
the necessity of its wandering about outside the tomb
in search of food. It is clear from many texts that,
unless the double was supplied with sufficient food,

it would wander forth from the tomb and eat any kind
of offal and drink any kind of dirty water which it
might find in its path. But besides the shadow, and
the double, and the soul, the spirit of the deceased,
which usually had its abode in heaven, was sometimes
to be found in the tomb. There is, however, good
reason for stating that the immortal part of man which
lived in the tomb and had its special abode in the
statue of the deceased was the ",double." This is
proved by the fact that a special part of the tomb was
reserved for the *ka*, or double, which was called the "house
" of the *ka*," and that a priest, called the "priest of the
" *ka*," was specially appointed to minister therein. The
double enjoyed the smell of the incense which was
offered at certain times each year in the tomb, as well
as the flowers, and herbs, and meat, and drink; and the
statue of the deceased in which the double dwelt took
pleasure in all the various scenes which were painted
or sculptured on the walls of the various chambers of
the tomb, and enjoyed again all the delights which
his body had enjoyed upon earth. The *ka*, or double,
then, in very early times was, to all intents and purposes,
the ghost of the Egyptians. In later times the *khu*, or
" spirit," seems to have been identified with it, and there
are frequent allusions in the texts to the sanctity of the
offerings made to the *khu*, and to their territories, *i.e.*,
the districts in which their mummified bodies lie.

Whether there was any general belief that the *ka*

or *khu* could or did hold intercourse with his relatives or friends whom he left alive upon earth cannot be said, but an instance is known in which a husband complains to his wife, who has been dead for three years, of the troubles which she has brought upon him since her death. He describes his own merits and the good treatment which he had vouchsafed to her when she was alive, and declares that the evil with which she is requiting him is not to be endured. To make his complaint to reach her he first reduced it to writing upon papyrus, then went to her tomb and read it there, and finally tied the papyrus to a statue or figure of his wife which was therein; since her double or spirit lived in the tomb she would, of course, read the writing and understand it.[1] It is a pity that we have no means of knowing what was the result of the husband's complaint. Elsewhere[2] we have a fragment of a conversation which a priest of Amen called Khonsu-em-heb, who was searching for a suitable place in which to build his tomb, holds with the double or spirit of some person whom he has disturbed, and the spirit of the dead tells some details of his life to the living man. The cemeteries were regarded with awe by the ancient Egyptians because of the spirits of the dead

---

[1] For the text see Leemans, *Monuments Égyptiens*, Partie II., pll. 183, 184, Leyden, 1846, fol.; for a transcript into hieroglyphics see Maspero, *Journal Asiatique*, Sér. 7, tom. 15, May and June, 1880, pp. 365-420.

[2] See Golénischeff in *Recueil de Travaux*, tom. iii., pp. 3-7.

who dwelt in them, and even the Arabic-speaking peoples of Egypt and the Sûdân, if we exclude the "antiquity grubber," have them in great respect for the same reason.[1] The modern peoples of the Sûdân firmly believe that the spirits of those slain in battle dwell on the field where they fell, or where their bodies are buried, and the soldiers in the tenth battalion of Lord Kitchener's army declare that the grave of the gallant Major Sidney, who was shot while charging at the head of his regiment, in the battle of Abū Hamed, August 7th, 1897, "is watched regularly "every night by the ghosts of the native soldiers who "were killed at Abū Hamed, and who mount guard "over their dead commander's tomb, challenging, with "every military detail, all passers-by. So implicitly "is this legend credited by the blacks that none of

[1] When I visited the Pyramids of Meroë in 1898 I took with me the local *shēkh*, and a man and a boy to look after the donkeys. Having come to within half a mile of the pyramids the three stopped and wished me to ride on by myself, and when I asked them why they did not want to come up the hill to the pyramids with me the *shēkh* replied that they had been built by kings whose spirits still dwelt there, and that it would not be seemly for him and his companions to "trouble" them. I pressed him to come, but he answered, "It is not "the custom of our country to go there," so I walked on by myself. When I had been in the pyramid field for about two hours taking photographs and measurements, the *shēkh* arrived with the boy, but nothing would persuade him to walk about there, and having seated himself he recited prayers from the *Koran* in an undertone, and at intervals urged me to return to his straw house on the river bank as soon as possible. He was firmly convinced that the prismatic compass which I used was a talisman, and when he reached home he thanked God fervently that he had not been molested by the spirits of the dead.

"them will, after dusk, approach the grave. Any one
"doing so is believed to be promptly halted by a phan-
"tom sentry, and even the words (in Arabic), 'Guard,
"turn out!' are often (so the story goes) plainly heard
"repeated at some distance off across the desert." [1]

[1] See the illustrated paper *The Sketch*, No. 332, June 7, 1899,
p. 277. The following from the *Times* of July 7, 1899, is worth
quoting :—

"THE GRAVE OF A BRITISH NAVAL OFFICER IN JAPAN.—Recently a
" report came to the ears of the British Consul at Hiogo that the grave
"of a British naval officer existed near a village on the island of
"Hiroshima, in the Inland Sea of Japan—a place rarely visited by
"any foreigner—and that, for some reason, it was carefully kept in
"order by the peasants in the neighbourhood. The Consul accord-
"ingly communicated with the Governor of the prefecture in which
"the island is situated; inquiries were made, and the Governor was
"able to send to the Consul a history of the lonely grave. The story
"was appended by the Governor to a formal despatch of his own, and
"was obviously drawn up by the village headman or some equally
"humble official, and it is worth giving in full. The *Sylvia*, the
"vessel mentioned, was for many years engaged in surveying off the
"coasts of Japan:—'In the first year of Meiji, corresponding to
"A.D. 1868, H.B.M.S. *Sylvia* was proceeding on a voyage through the
"Inland Sea when an officer on board, named Lake, fell ill. He was
"landed on the island of Hiroshima, at the village of Hiroshima, in
"the district of Naka, province of Sanuki, and prefecture of Kagawa.
"The *Sylvia* proceeded along the coast of Hiroshima and cast anchor
"at Enoura Bay, to await the officer's recovery. In a few days, how-
"ever, he died, and Captain St. John buried his remains in ground
"belonging to the temple of Ikwoji above Enoura shrine, and, having
"set up a wooden cross to mark the grave, departed. Several years
"afterwards, when this monument had almost decayed from the effects
"of wind and rain, frost and snow, Awaburi Tokwan, Superior of
"Ikwoji Temple, and others said :—"Truly it would be too sad if
"the grave of our solitary guest from afar, who has become a spirit
"in a strange land, were suffered to pass out of all knowledge."
"Thereupon Terawaki Kaemon, head of a village guild, and other
"sympathisers, such as Oka Ryohaku, set on foot a scheme for the
"erection of a stone monument, and, the shore folk all with one accord

Q

The Egyptians believed that a man's fate or destiny was decided before he was born, and that he had no power whatever to alter it. Their sages, however, professed to be able to declare what the fate might be, provided that they were given certain data, that is to say, if they were told the date of his birth, and if they were able to ascertain the position of the planets and stars at that time. The goddess of fate or destiny was called " Shai," and she is usually accompanied by another goddess called " Renenet," who is commonly regarded as the lady of fortune; they both appear in the Judgment Scene, where they seem to watch the weighing of the heart on behalf of the deceased. But another goddess, Meskhenet, is sometimes present, and she also seems to have had influence over a man's future; in any case she was able to predict what that future was to be. Thus we read that she and Isis, and Nephthys, and Heqet, disguised as women, went to the house of Rā-user, whose wife Rut-Tettet was in travail; when they had been taken into her room they assisted her in giving birth to triplets, and as each child was born Meskhenet declared, "He shall be " a king who shall have dominion over the whole land."

"lending their help, the work was finally brought to completion.
"This was on the 7th day of the eleventh month of the fourth year
"of Meiji—that is, 1871. Since then nearly 30 winters have passed,
"during which time the islanders have not neglected to take good
"care of the tomb. In particular, from the 10th to the 16th day of
"the seventh month, old style, there are still persons found who every
"year clean and sweep the grave, and, offering up flowers and incense,
"mourn for and console the spirit of the dead.'"

And this prophecy was fulfilled, for the three boys
became three of the kings of the Vth dynasty.[1] The
Seven Hathor goddesses also could predict the future
of a human being, for in the well-known "Tale of
"Two Brothers" it is related that, when the god
Khnemu, at the request of Rā-Harmachis, had created
for Bata a wife "who was more beautiful in her person
"than any other woman in all the earth, for the essence
"of every god was contained in her," they came to see
her, and that they spake with one voice, saying, "Her
"death will be caused by the knife." And this came
to pass, for, according to the story, when the king
whose wife she became heard from her first husband
that she had left him and had wrought evil against
him, he entered into judgment with her in the presence
of his chiefs and nobles, and "one carried out their
"decree," *i.e.*, they sentenced her to death and she was
executed.   Similarly, in another story, the Seven
Hathors came to see the son who had been born to
a certain king in answer to his prayers to the gods,
and when they had seen him they said, "He shall die
"by means of a crocodile, or a serpent, or a dog." The
story goes on to say how he escaped from the crocodile
and the serpent, and though the end is wanting, it is
quite clear that he was wounded by an accidental bite
of his dog and so died.[2]   The moral of all such stories

[1] See Erman, *Westcar Papyrus,* Berlin, 1890, hieroglyphic transcript,
pll. 9 and 10.
[2] See Maspero, *Contes Égyptiens,* pp. 29–46.

is that there is no possibility of avoiding fate, and it is most probable that the modern Egyptian has only inherited his ancestors' views as to its immutability.[1] A man's life might, however, be happy or unhappy according as the hour of the day or the day itself was lucky or unlucky, and every day of the Egyptian year was divided into three parts, each of which was lucky or unlucky. When Olympias was about to give birth to Alexander the Great, Nectanebus stood by her making observations of the heavenly bodies, and from time to time he besought her to restrain herself until the auspicious hour had arrived ; and it was not until he saw a certain splendour in the sky and knew that all the heavenly bodies were in a favourable position that he permitted her to bring forth her child. And when he had said, "O queen, now thou wilt give birth "to a governor of the world," the child fell upon the ground while the earth quaked, and the lightnings flashed, and the thunder roared.[2] Thus it is quite evident that the future of a child depended even upon the hour in which he was born.

In magical papyri we are often told not to perform certain magical ceremonies on such and such days, the idea being that on these days hostile powers will make them to be powerless, and that gods mightier than

---

[1] The uneducated Muhammadan believes that man's fate is written upon his skull, and that the sutures are the writing. No man, however, can read them. See the words of Zayn al-Mawasif in Burton's *Alf Laylah wa Laylah*, vol. viii., p. 237.

[2] See Pseudo-Callisthenes, I. 12.

those to which the petitioner would appeal will be in the ascendant. There have come down to us, fortunately, papyri containing copies of the Egyptian calendar, in which each third of every day for three hundred and sixty days of the year is marked lucky or unlucky, and we know from other papyri *why* certain days were lucky or unlucky, and why others were only partly so. Taking the month Thoth, which was the first month of the Egyptian year, and began, according to the Gregorian Calendar, on August 29th, we find that the days are marked as follows:—

Day		Day		Day	
Day 1		Day 11		Day 21	
„ 2		„ 12		„ 22	
„ 3		„ 13	(*sic*)	„ 23	
„ 4		„ 14		„ 24	
„ 5		„ 15		„ 25	
„ 6		„ 16		„ 26	
„ 7		„ 17		„ 27	
„ 8		„ 18		„ 28	
„ 9		„ 19		„ 29	
„ 10		„ 20		„ 30	[1]

[1] See Brit. Mus. Papyrus, No. 10,474.

Now the sign ⌇ means "lucky," and ⌇ means "unlucky"; thus at a glance it could be seen which third of the day is lucky or unlucky, and the man who consulted the calendar would, of course, act accordingly. It must be noted that the priests or magicians who drew up the calendar had good reasons for their classification of the days, as we may see from the following example. The 19th day of Thoth is, in the above list, marked wholly lucky, *i.e.*, each third of it is lucky, and the papyrus Sallier IV.[1] also marks it wholly lucky, and adds the reason:—"It is a day of "festival in heaven and upon earth in the presence "of Rā. It is the day when flame was hurled upon "those who followed the boat containing the shrine "of the gods; and on this day the gods gave praises "being content," etc. But in both lists the 26th day is marked wholly unlucky, the reason being, "This was "the day of the fight between Horus and Set." They first fought in the form of men, then they took the form of bears, and in this state did battle with each other for three days and three nights. Isis aided Set when he was getting the worst in the fight, and Horus thereupon cut off his mother's head, which Thoth transformed by his words of power into that of a cow and put on her body. On this day offerings are to be made to Osiris and Thoth, but work of any kind is absolutely forbidden. The calendars of lucky

[1] See Chabas, *Le Calendrier*, p. 24.

and unlucky days do not, however, always agree as to a given day. Thus in the list given above the 20th day of Thoth is marked wholly unlucky, but in the papyrus Sallier IV. it is wholly lucky, but the reader is told not to do any work in it, nor to slay oxen, nor to receive a stranger; on this day the gods who are in the following of Rā slew the rebels. Concerning the fourth day of the next month, Paophi, the papyrus Sallier IV. says, " Go not forth from thy house from any side of it; " whosoever is born on this day shall die of the disease " *aat.*" Concerning the fifth day it says, " Go not forth " from thy house from any side of it, and hold no " intercourse with women. This is the day wherein all " things were performed in the divine presence, and the " majesty of the god Menthu was satisfied therein. " Whosoever is born on this day shall die of excessive " venery." Concerning the ninth day it says, " Who- " soever is born on this day shall die of old age," and concerning the fifteenth, " Go not forth from thy " dwelling at eventide, for the serpent Uatch, the son of " the god, goeth forth at this time, and misfortunes " follow him; whosoever shall see him shall lose his " eye straightway." Again, the twenty-sixth day of Paophi was a lucky day for making the plan of a house; on the fifth day of Hathor no fire was to be kindled in the house; on the sixteenth day it was forbidden to listen to songs of joy because on this day Isis and Nephthys wept for Osiris at Abydos;

a man born on the twenty-third day would die by
drowning; and so on. But to the three hundred and
sixty days given in the calendars of lucky and unlucky
days must be added the five epagomenal days which
were considered to be of great importance and had
each its peculiar name. On the first Osiris was born,
on the second Heru-ur (Aroueris), on the third Set, on
the fourth Isis, and on the fifth Nephthys; the first,
third, and fifth of these days were unlucky, and no
work of any kind was to be undertaken on them. The
rubric which refers to these days[1] states that whosoever
knoweth their names shall never suffer from thirst, that
he shall never be smitten down by disease, and that the
goddess Sekhet[2] shall never take possession of him;
it also directs that figures of the five gods mentioned
above shall be drawn with unguent and *ānti* scent
upon a piece of fine linen, evidently to serve as an
amulet.

From the life of Alexander the Great by Pseudo-
Callisthenes[3] we learn that the Egyptians were skilled
in the art of casting nativities, and that knowing the
exact moment of the birth of a man they proceeded to
construct his horoscope. Nectanebus employed for the
purpose a tablet made of gold and silver and acacia
wood, to which were fitted three belts. Upon the

[1] See Chabas, *op. cit.*, p. 104.
[2] The Eye of Sekhet seems to have taken the form of noxious
vapours in the fields at sunrise; see Chabas, *op. cit.*, p. 78.
[3] I. 4.

outer belt was Zeus with the thirty-six *decani* surrounding him; upon the second the twelve signs of
the Zodiac were represented; and upon the third the
sun and moon.[1] He set the tablet upon a tripod, and
then emptied out of a small box upon it models of
the seven stars [2] that were in the belts, and put into
the middle belt eight precious stones; these he arranged
in the places wherein he supposed the planets which
they represented would be at the time of the birth
of Olympias, and then told her fortune from them.
But the use of the horoscope is much older than the
time of Alexander the Great, for to a Greek horoscope [3]
in the British Museum is attached "an introductory
"letter from some master of the art of astrology to
"his pupil, named Hermon, urging him to be very
"exact and careful in his application of the laws which
"the ancient Egyptians, with their laborious devotion
"to the art, had discovered and handed down to
"posterity." Thus we have good reason for assigning
the birthplace of the horoscope to Egypt. In connexion with the horoscope must be mentioned the
"sphere" or "table" of Democritus as a means of
making predictions as to life and death. In a magical

---

[1] I quote from my History of *Alexander the Great*, Cambridge,
1889, p. 5.

[2] *I.e.*, Sun, Moon, Zeus, Kronos, Aphrodite, and Hermes; we must
add Mars according to Meusel's Greek text.

[3] Published for the first time by Kenyon, *Catalogue of Greek Papyri*
vol. i. p. 132 ff.

papyrus[1] we are told to " ascertain in what month the " sick man took to his bed, and the name he received " at his birth. Calculate the [course of] the moon, " and see how many periods of thirty days have " elapsed; then note in the table the number of days " left over, and if the number comes in the upper " part of the table, he will live, but if in the lower " part, he will die."

THE TABLE.

1	10	19
2	11	20
3	13	23
4	14	25
7	16	26
9	17	27
5	15	22
6	18	28
8	21	29
12	24	30

Both from the religious and profane literature of Egypt we learn that the gods and man in the future life were able at will to assume the form of any animal, or bird, or plant, or living thing, which they pleased, and one of the greatest delights to which a man looked forward was the possession of that power. This is proved by the fact that no less than twelve[2] of the chapters of the Book of the Dead are devoted to

[1] *Leyden Pap. V.* (ed. Leemans), col. xi., l. 1 ff.
[2] *I.e.*, Chapters LXXVII. to LXXXVIII.

providing the deceased with the words of power, the recital of which was necessary to enable him to transform himself into a "hawk of gold," a "divine hawk," "the governor of the sovereign princes," "the god who "giveth light in the darkness," a lotus, the god Ptah, a *bennu* bird (*i.e.*, phœnix), a heron, a "living soul," a swallow, the serpent Sata, and a crocodile; and another chapter[1] enabled him to transform himself into "whatever form he pleaseth." Armed with this power he could live in the water in the form of a crocodile, in the form of a serpent he could glide over the rocks and ground, in the form of the birds mentioned above he could fly through the air, and · soar up and perch himself upon the bow of the boat of Rā, in the form of the lotus he had mastery over the plants of the field, and in the form of Ptah he became "more "powerful than the lord of time, and shall gain the "mastery over millions of years." The *bennu* bird, it will be remembered, was said to be the "soul of Rā," and by assuming this form the deceased identified himself with Khepera, the great god of creation, and thus acquired the attributes of the soul of the Sun-god. In the Elysian Fields he was able to assume any form and to swim and fly to any distance in any direction. It is noteworthy that no beast of the field or wild animal is mentioned as a type of his possible transformations into animals.

[1] *I.e.*, Chapter LXXVI.

Now the Egyptians believed that as the souls of the departed could assume the form of any living thing or plant, so the "gods," who in many respects closely resembled them, could and did take upon themselves the forms of birds and beasts; this was the fundamental idea of the so-called "Egyptian animal worship," which provoked the merriment of the cultured Greek, and drew down upon the Egyptians the ridicule and abuse of the early Christian writers. But if the matter be examined closely its apparent stupidity disappears. The Egyptians paid honour to certain birds, and animals, and reptiles, because they considered that they possessed certain of the characteristics of the gods to whom they made them sacred. The bull was a type of the strength and procreative power of the god of reproduction in nature, and the cow was the type of his female counterpart; every sacred animal and living thing possessed some quality or attribute which was ascribed to some god, and as each god was only a form of Rā, the quality or attribute ascribed to him was that of the Sun-god himself. The educated Egyptian never worshipped an animal as an animal, but only as an incarnation of a god, and the reverence paid to animals in Egypt was in no way different from that paid to the king who was regarded as "divine" and as an incarnation of Rā the Sun-god, who was the visible symbol of the Creator. The relation of the king to Rā was identical with that of Rā to God. The

Hebrews, Greeks, and Romans never understood the logical conception which underlay the reverence with which the Egyptians regarded certain animals, and as a result they grossly misrepresented their religion. The ignorant people, no doubt, often mistook the symbol for what it symbolized, but it is wrong to say that the Egyptians worshipped animals in the ordinary sense of the word, and this fact cannot be too strongly insisted on. Holding the views he did about transformations there was nothing absurd in the reverence which the Egyptian paid to animals. When a sacred animal died the god whom it represented sought out another animal of the same species in which to renew his incarnation, and the dead body of the animal, inasmuch as it had once been the dwelling-place of a god, was mummified and treated in much the same way as a human body after death, in order that it might enjoy immortality. These views seem strange, no doubt, to us when judged by modern ideas, but they formed an integral part of the religious beliefs of the Egyptians, from the earliest to the latest times. What is remarkable, however, is the fact that, in spite of invasions, and foreign wars, and internal dissensions, and external influences of all kinds, the Egyptians clung to their gods and the some-times childish and illogical methods which they adopted in serving them with a conservatism and zeal which have earned for them the reputation of being at once the most religious and most superstitious nation of antiquity. Whatever literary treasures may be brought to light in the future as the result of excavations in Egypt, it is most improbable that we shall ever receive from that country any ancient Egyptian work which can properly be classed among the literature of atheism or freethought; the Egyptian might be more or less religious according to his nature and temperament, but, judging from the writings of his priests and teachers which are now in our hands, the man who was without religion and God in some form or other was most rare, if not unknown.

THE END.